Nehemiah Adams

Agnes and the little key

Bereaved parents instructed and comforted. Tenth Edition

Nehemiah Adams

Agnes and the little key
Bereaved parents instructed and comforted. Tenth Edition

ISBN/EAN: 9783337268862

Printed in Europe, USA, Canada, Australia, Japan

Cover: Foto ©Andreas Hilbeck / pixelio.de

More available books at **www.hansebooks.com**

AGNES

AND THE LITTLE KEY:

OR,

BEREAVED PARENTS INSTRUCTED AND COMFORTED.

BY

NEHEMIAH ADAMS, D.D.,
BOSTON.

TENTH EDITION, REVISED.

BOSTON:

D. LOTHROP AND COMPANY,

FRANKLIN ST., COR. OF HAWLEY.

PUBLISHERS' PREFACE TO THE TENTH EDITION.

We are assured by the author of this book, that, in view of the sacredly private experiences which it contains, it would not have been published had he not supposed that special pains to conceal the authorship would be successful. On being published, the book was by common consent and without question ascribed to its true source. We have hitherto yielded to the author's wish in withholding his name from the title-page.

The book was soon, without any suggestion from this country, printed in London. The Rt. Rev. Archibald Campbell, Bishop of London, now Archbishop of Canterbury, had about that time excited the Christian sympathy of the British public by great domestic bereavements. The London publishers sought permission to dedicate the English edition of this book to him, which was done as follows : —

"To the Right Hon. and Right Rev. ARCHIBALD CAMPBELL, Lord Bishop of London, himself an earnest laborer in the field of Christian love, this volume, written by one who desires to impart to others the strength and consolation and hope vouchsafed to him in the house of mourning, is, by his Lordship's kind permission, most respectfully dedicated."

The author of " Memorials of Captain Hedley Vicars "
wrote a Preface to this English edition, from which the
following is extracted : —

" A stranger to the author of this book, his name even un-
known to me, I feel it to be almost a sacrilege to comply with
the request to write a Preface for it ; fearing lest any touch of
mine should mar the delicacy, simplicity, and beauty of this
memorial monument. . . . A single glance at these pages
would have been introduction enough for the volume to mourners on this side of the Atlantic. It is the tone of simple truth,
the reality, in this record of an earthly sorrow gradually gilded
and finally glorified by a Heavenly Hope and Faith, which
renders it peculiarly suitable to mourners. . . . There is none
of that dry, theological consolation, or hard, unsympathizing
denunciation of all impassioned grief, too frequently assumed
in books written for mourners. . . . He has spoken to his
brothers and sisters throughout a mourning world. . . . It is a
record of reaping in joy after sowing in tears."

"The Apostle Poule unto the Romaines writeth, Man shall rejoice with hem that maketh joye, and wepen with swiche folke as wepen."

Chaucer.

CONTENTS.

CHAPTER VII.

CHAPTER VIII.

CHAPTER IX.

CHAPTER X.

CHAPTER XI.

AGNES.

CHAPTER I.

AGNES. — HER SICKNESS, DEATH, AND BURIAL. — FINDING OF THE KEY.

SHE was not quite one year old. I cannot venture to describe her. My heart swells and is ready to break at the thought of some sweet, touching feature, some winning way, the posture and motion of her hands or feet, her inarticulate noises with her lips, the pressure of her mouth against our cheeks, that being as far as she had advanced in kissing. Sights of her asleep, when her mother and I stood over her with lamp in hand, are as deeply stamped on my mind as views in the Alps. I could tell you every dimple which we detected as she lay on her back, a knee or arm disengaged from her clothing. All her mimicry of sounds and of motions, and her little feats, which astonished herself and made us shout; her morning bath, she a little image, with her very straight back, plashing the water with her feet; and other nameless things, raise the question and leave it in doubt, whether I wish there were more of them to remember, or whether it is well for me that she had been developed no more. Human bliss arrives at perfection as frequently in such scenes and experiences, as when we have made calculations for happiness; indeed, we are never more happy than during the little, sudden tournaments of love with a young child: and the man who has a wife and child supplying him with these inadvertent pleasures, will find in the retrospect that he was most happy when he least suspected it. To know when we have in possession the means of true happiness, and to rejoice in it, and feel satisfied, is rare. Would that I had thought more of this when my little child was with me !

Sometimes I looked at her with a feeling of awe. Mine, indeed, she was ; but. in what a subcrdinate sense! That perfect frame, that wondrous mind, that immortal destiny, often made me shrink into nothingness at the contemplation of her, — feeling that God, in making her, had rolled a sphere into an orbit which is measureless, making it touch mine, but having a path of its own which cannot be comprehended in that of another, not even in that of the earthly parent. I was glad that there was an infinite God to possess this infinite treasure, and control it; for it was too much for me. My enjoyment of her was often overshadowed by these thoughts. Still she was to me a perfect joy. Her beautifully unfolding life left me nothing to desire.

But the destroyer came. It had been an exceedingly hot summer, and cholera infantum began to waste the little face and frame. We saw that she must die; we nevertheless main-

tained a cheerfulness of feeling which afterward seemed to us unnatural; but no doubt it
was kindly given, to bear us through the trial.
The last night that she was put to rest, her
symptoms were favorable; but, early in the
morning, the nurse whispered to me, that the
child "looked strange;" and she led my way
to the nursery. The little patient lay with
her hand under her cheek; her eyes were
raised and fixed on the wall. I supposed that
she was watching a shadow, and I spoke to
her by name. She did not move, nor did she
turn her eyes. I spoke again, and kissed her;
it was vain; the fearful truth flashed upon
me that she was convulsed. We watched
her till sundown, when she ceased to breathe.

I fear that some of you will smile if I say
she seemed to me the sweetest little thing
that ever died; that, as she lay in her last
sleep, no sight could be quite so beautiful and
touching; that the loss of a child never,
probably, awoke such tenderness of love and
such grief. Suffer me at least to think so,
without debate.

How can I tell you any thing about the last
sad scene at the grave? Enough to say that
each of us kissed the sweet face; we gazed on
her a few moments, while tears ran down; and
some things were uttered between speaking
and crying, till at length her mother kneeled
and held her face near the little face for a
few moments, without a sound; then drew
the white embroidered blanket over the little
thing, for it was a cold day; and thus the last
" Now I lay me down to sleep " seemed to be
said and heard. I closed the lid. " Lieth
down and riseth not, till the heavens be no
more;"— what shall I have seen and known
before I see this face again! That simple
thing, the closing of the lid, what a world of
meaning was in it! My thoughts were making a whirlpool about me, till my eye was
taken by the nearer approach of a man, in
his shirt-sleeves and rough working garb,
who respectfully seemed to intimate, We
are ready, sir, when you are. Oh! must we,
must we part? Must the grave have her?

With an effort, I said, "Thy will be done." I turned the key, and took it out of the lock, and understood how even good men could have opened their mouths, at certain times, against the day of their birth. We waited. In a few moments, one more little mound grew up from the earth; the clods of the valley had become sweet to one more father and mother.

We rode away. I was glad that the horses started off so fast, though, for the first moment, it shocked me. I was expecting to move away at the slow, solemn pace with which we came.

Turning a corner in the cemetery, a little stone over a little grave, the only one in the enclosure, caught my eye, as we drove past, with this inscription : CHARLIE. Ah, is Charlie dead ? I felt very sorry. Who Charlie was, I did not know ; but his father, I thought, had been there on an errand like mine. Had I met him in the street, on my way home, some one pointing him out to me, I would have stopped him, and told him what I had seen, and that Agnes was dead. For a moment, the stream of my grief was broken and divided by that little headstone, as a great river is divided by the delta at its mouth; but it came together again very soon.

It is known, and some of you to whom I speak have had painful opportunity to know, that there has been, of late years, an improvement in the little depositories in which we convey the forms of infants and young children to their last resting-place.

Their shape is not in seeming mockery of the rigid, swathed body; the broken lines and angles of the old coffin are drawn into continuous lines; they look like other things, and not like that which looks like nothing else, a coffin; you would be willing to have such a shape for the depository of any household article. Within, they are prepared with a pearly-white lining; the inside of the lid is draped in the same way; the name is on the inside; and a lock and key supplant the remorseless screws and screw-driver.

As I was going to bed that night, and was taking off my vest, emptying the pockets, in a listless mood, of whatever had found its way there through the day, I drew forth, among other things, a little key, trimmed with white satin ribbon.

Then the clouds returned after the rain. I thought, for a few moments, that I should lose my reason.

Why need I attempt to relate the mingled feelings, with a particular anguish in each of them, with which I stood in the middle of my room, alone, holding that key in my hand?

It became necessary, at last, to put it somewhere. But it was the most difficult thing to dispose of which ever came into my possession. I could neither keep it, nor part with it. I abhorred it, and idolized it. I wished to be rid of it, and I clung to it. There was a fearful spell about it; and yet it was a charm, a precious treasure, and at the same time a symbol of my agony. I hung it up over a picture in my private room, for the night.

But I lay some time in the morning, afraid
to go into that room. I felt that there was
but one thing there. I opened the door, with
my eyes levelled at the spot where I was to
see that thing. The cheerful sunlight was
streaming upon that part of the room, and,
how strange! it made a focus on the key, and
the light gleamed from it. I ought to have
felt, more than I did, that the love and compassion of God were trying to speak comfort
to me.

I took the key, and wrote the little name
on the ribbon, the birth-day, the dying-day,
the day of burial, the path, and the number
of the burial-place.

Enhancing the value of this priceless treasure by this inscription, I consulted with
myself what to do with it. Perhaps you
would kindly be willing to follow me in my
perplexity, and see how one project after
another arose and was debated in my mind
in settling the question where I should place
and keep the little key. Though you suffer

2

the afflicted to tell their tale in their own
way, with all its needless particularity of
dates, incidents, and strictest regard to un
important historical succession, I shall avoid
these things, for I know to whom I speak.   A
goodly company have I with me, sitting on
the ground, keeping silence, and hearkening
to my woe.

CHAPTER II.

WHAT SHALL I DO WITH THE KEY?

THE question was, "What shall I do with the key of the little coffin?"

A large part of the forenoon was spent, to the neglect of other things, in fruitless debates with myself as to the best way of keeping this strange possession. I had, perhaps, thirty keys, but never was I at a loss where to keep any of them. Most of them were in bunches, on rings; the thought of placing this among them was revolting. I was afraid of seeing it too often, while I also wished to keep it constantly in sight. Should I desecrate the key of such an enclosure, as I would, by mixing it with drawer-keys and keys of trunks?

My first conclusion was, that I should keep

it in my purse. Then I resolved that I would
tie it in my Bible. How it would unlock for
me the promises of God's word, open many
meanings of passages which I never thought
of, and be a seal to all the truths which would
meet my eye, especially those relating to the
transitoriness of earthly good, and to all which
is said of heaven. And yet I was afraid of
seeing it too often.

The little crib had been carried away to the
store-chamber, with the trunks, old andirons,
carpets, and supernumerary things. To tie the
little key to the little crib, joining her first
and last resting-places together, was another
project, which was soon abandoned.

"I will store it up with her playthings," I
said to myself; and went to the drawer of the
old "secretary" in the upper chamber, and
looked upon them.

I did wrong to trust myself there. My
wife, with the child in her lap, was riding with
me in the time of apple-blossoms, through
some of the neighboring towns; and stop

ping a peddler under a great apple-tree, and seeing the rattle, she took it, for future use. How the blossom-leaves fell into the chaise, and on our laps, while a little hand was made to open, and was held out to catch some of them. O that incense-breathing May day! that sweet communion, that joint love for the little treasure with us, which made us the happiest of parents! And now I had come to lay the little key by the side of that toy. Sir Thomas Browne says, "Fortune lays the plot of our adversities in the foundation of our felicities." How did those playthings seem to look up in my face and mock me! The strings of red coral to loop the arms of dresses were there in the same white satin paper-box in which I brought them from the jeweller's. I was duly notified and was present when they were tried on. A tin horse on rockers, red and white, lay prostrate on his side. Two india-rubber rings, with prints of small teeth in them, were there. What searchings for those teeth there used to be, before they came up like lambs from the washing. A box with a puff-ball and powder was there put away; a silver whistle, with small bells at the end; a Turkish-looking head and body on a stick, with spangles on pendant strips of cashmere; a little comb and very soft brush, all lay together, as though discrimination had dreaded to exercise itself there. And so in reckless negligence, incongruous things, bound together, however, by one dread tie, lay useless and neglected. Here seemed the place for the little key, except that it involved the idea of abandoning it. Had its use come to an end? shall it be doomed to oblivion? shall I put it where I shall not dare to look at it, through fear of meeting other things which will combine their power to torment me? I can look at it alone. But I could neither consent to leave it where I would not be willing to go, or where, if I did go, I should suffer at the sight of so many other little memorials. So I brought it away, as much at a loss as ever how to dispose of it.

By this time it became necessary for me to take advice on the subject; and accordingly I went into my wife's room, and found her sitting before her cheerful, blazing fire, the room darkened a little, and her small Bible lying in her lap, which she had evidently been reading when I tapped at her door.

What a hush there was in that chamber of sorrow! Things seemed to be holding their peace; they looked as though they had settled themselves into a posture for deep thought. The muslin window-curtains never hung so straight and proper before. The chairs each had a vacated look, while the cannel coal made its sizzling noises more vivaciously than ever, and, as I fancied, with the feelings of a boy whistling in the dark.

Dear wife! she was pale, and had been weeping. May I not as well disclose the dread secret here as elsewhere, that now she sleeps by the side of Agnes? I will not enlarge. I sat by her side, and we both looked into the fire.

"You did not take cold yesterday," said I.

"No," said she; "it was thoughtful in you to fix that board for me to stand on while they were filling the "—

There was a pause, and I said, "Let us try and not think of yesterday;"—at the same time knowing how foolish it was to say this, especially as I myself thought of nothing else; but I had to say something.

"Will you tell me," said I, "what you were saying, yesterday, when you put your face down to the dear little face at the grave, and held it there?"

"Oh, I recollected," said she, "how I gave that child to God before she was born. One day I read that passage in the Psalms where David is dwelling with so much satisfaction on God's perfect knowledge of him, and 'possessing' him before he was born."

I sat and thought of those words, which we seldom repeat to one another; or, if we read them in company, the voice feels a subduing influence from them. Yet, to one in trouble,

nothing gives a more impressive sense of
God's perfect knowledge of him, and property
in him, than to read, "Thine eyes did see my
substance, yet being unperfect; and in thy
book all my members were written, which in
continuance were fashioned, when as yet
there was none of them. How precious, also,
are thy thoughts unto me, O God! how
great is the sum of them! If I should count
them, they are more in number than the
sand : when I awake I am still with thee."

She broke my reverie by saying, "At the
time you refer to, yesterday, I was going over
my feelings about Agnes, from the very first
moment, and all along; and I thought how entirely I gave her up to God, when I knew that
I was again to be a mother, and when she was
given to us. When I took my last look, and
felt her little cheek for the last time, I did
again, what I had done so many times before,
— I gave er up to God, to be disposed of for
his glory.

"And now," said I, "he has taken us at our
word."

"If we were sincere in all that we did," she replied, "we have nothing to regret. Though her child lay dead, the Shunamite woman said, 'It is well.' I am trying to say this, and you must help me."

"I came in," said I, "to ask what we should do with that little key which I brought away with me yesterday."

"Oh! did you bring it away? I wondered whether you did. I almost hoped that you gave it to the undertaker."

"What could he have done with it?" said I.

"It could never be of any use, of course, and why should you keep it? I am afraid it will only harrow up your feelings."

"Perhaps, then," I replied, "I will take it to him, and let him mix it with other keys of the same kind, or use it as a spare key when one is lost."

"Oh, no!" she said hesitatingly: "I would not do that."

"But where," said I, "shall we keep it?" I then told her of my several projects, and how it had made me suffer already, and still how I clung to the little treasure.

She had the greatest skill in managing my feelings, at all times, without any show of power over me. I worshipped her almost as a superior being, leading, guiding me in times of great excitement, and always bringing me out with self-respect and with augmented reverence for her.

"Before you discuss the little key," she said, "I want you to read to me that long letter which Mr. W. wrote soon after Agnes was born. I always wondered why Mr. W. never tried his hand at writing tales. That story is told in such a way that it affects me exceedingly. It will divert my mind to hear you read it; and, at the same time, it is on a subject which will suit my feelings."

I went to my desk for the manuscript, asking myself whether it was really for her sake or my own, that she wished me to read it to her; and, though I suspected that it was for my sake, yet the ingenious way in which it

was brought about pleased me, and I gladly
gave myself up to the innocent stratagem, —
if, indeed, it were such.   As I took the manuscript from the file of papers which were with
it, I slipped the little key under the large
india-rubber band which held them together,
glad of some temporary hiding-place for it.

The dinner-bell rang on my way back to
her room.   "Is it possible?" we both ex-
claimed: "where has the morning gone?"   I
thought it was about noon.   It was two
o'clock.

CHAPTER III.

ENTERING the dining-room together, we found our chairs set for us at the table, as usual, and between them a high chair. Jane had followed her habit of placing the little chair at table. We both uttered something like a groan, and sat down; but it was some time before I could speak audibly enough to ask a blessing. She was regularly brought in with the dessert, tied into her high chair, and then began the chief pleasure of our meal. Her little body was kept in exultant action; the table was thumped and beaten; and, as the things rattled, she felt encouraged to pound the more. The oranges excited her desire; and, reaching and stretching after them with a straining noise in her throat, her face would

29

grow red, till her determination was soothed
by her effort to say "please," or something
which was accepted as an equivalent, when
her effort to grasp and hold the orange which
was rolled toward her proving, literally, fruitless, she made us laugh at her, she striving to
laugh as loud as we.

The chair kept its place during the meal,
and tears were our meat, till my wife essayed
to be my comforter, and said, —

"We are not the only parents who have
gone through such trials."

"How little we have, after all," said I, "to
weep over, compared with many! There are
trials with living children which are worse
than losing an infant. But do you not think
that the death of a dear little child is a very
peculiar sorrow? It seems to me that I have
seen people in more anguish under the loss
of little children than in any other affliction."

"Oh!" said she, "there is an exquisite tenderness in your love for a little child which
makes the affliction peculiar. After all, it is

my intense love for Agnes which distresses
me."

"It is so with me; but I suppose," said I,
"that a mother has feelings toward the child
when it is gone, which, in some respects, are
different from those which fathers have; and
yet, sometimes, I think that I am suffering
more than you, or that you have more control
over your feelings than I."

"We must help each other," said she; "but
a daughter is a great comfort to a mother, as
she grows up, and is company for her at
home. I hardly know what to do with myself; it seems as though I had nothing to do;
but that is not right; I mean to feel differ-
ently; but I suppose we must expect to suffer
for a time."

"There is 'a time to embrace, and a time
to refrain from embracing,' the wise man tells
us. But," said I, "let us resolve on this, that
we will not let sorrow make us selfish. Some
people are wholly absorbed for a long
time in their sorrow, and become unfit for

every thing. Let us try and make our hearts expand, instead of curling their affections inwardly, and shutting themselves up closer from others."

" It seems to me," she said, " as though I should greatly love every mother now, and her child, and do all in my power to comfort those who lose children. I am so glad that I do not find it in my heart to murmur against God. Some people seem to me to retain an unforgiving spirit against God when he takes a child from them."

I told her of a mother, who, on losing an only child, said to me, "I don't see why I should be singled out, and be robbed of my only child, when my sisters each have large families, and have never lost a child." My blood ran cold to hear the woman talk so. I could not help thinking, It may be God loves you most, and therefore afflicts you. Oh! when we part with our perfect confidence in God's goodness and wisdom, we drift, without help or hold, we know not where.

In the course of our talk, I related two anecdotes. A former President of the College in Cambridge, Mass., when he was pastor of a church, called on a lady who had lost a child, and who took occasion to say many things which manifested a quarrelsome disposition, or certainly an unsubmissive state of feeling. She "never could be reconciled;" she "never would submit to it;" it was "more than human nature could bear." Her pastor silently heard her through; and, after a short pause, he quietly said, "Well, madam, what do you propose to do about it?"

An English clergyman was praying at the bedside of a sick child; and, after petitioning for its recovery, in an earnest manner, he said, "But, if Thou hast otherwise ordained, and hast purposed to take away this child" —

"Oh, no!" interrupted the mother, "never; oh, don't say so! I cannot have it!" and so, more than once during the prayer, she protested audibly against the sovereign will of God. The clergyman was much pained and grieved at this want of submission to God's most holy will. He and that mother both lived to see that child perish on the gallows, by the hand of the public executioner, at the age of twenty-five.

"But," said I, "we have both thought and talked enough about this for the present; and so we will postpone our reading, and I will take you to drive this beautiful afternoon."

CHAPTER IV.

CONSOLATIONS.

BEFORE bringing the horse to the door, I walked to the post-office. On my way, I was struck with the manner of many of my friends and acquaintances. One thing affected me. Some, who hardly ever had felt sufficiently acquainted to bow as we passed, saluted me as I went by. They knew of my affliction; they noticed the weed on my hat; they saw my sorrow, probably, in my looks. It made me love my fellow-men more than ever; it made me resolve to be kind to people in trouble. Some of my acquaintances, who were formerly free to speak, went by with most respectful and solemn looks, unwilling to intrude upon my grief; while here and there a hand would grasp mine; and, with

eyes full of tears, one and another would say,
" Oh, my dear sir, I know all that you have
gone through, for I have felt the same." That
walk did much to change the complexion of
my feelings; but alas! every now and then I
thought of that little key, and of my morning's employment, and I felt as we do when
the sea swells under our feet.

As soon as we started on our drive, we met
young children in the arms of nursery-maids,
or in wicker carriages. We watched them as
they passed, as though they were strange or
most interesting sights. Once I turned the
horse and rode back, to give my wife a view
of a little face over a nurse's shoulder. " Dear
little thing," said she, "just the age of Agnes:
how happy her mother must be!"

" Are you not glad for her mother?" said I.

" Surely I am, and love her dearly, without
knowing her," she replied. "And one thing I
can hardly account for, — that seeing these
little things makes me love God more than
ever."

"Now, that is a good sign," said I; "for, when we love God, I do believe that afflictions make us love him more. We cannot be stationary in our feelings towards him in times of great sorrow: we either go back from him, and are cold towards him, which is a dreadful sign; or we cling to him, and say, 'Whom have I in heaven but thee?'"

"You praise me sometimes," said she, "when I wish that you would examine me, and tell me my faults."

"I examined you then," said I, "and felt bound to give the result. We must not deny the work of God's grace in us: that grieves him. We must discriminate in our confessions, and be thankful for any right feeling, and cherish it."

"What were those lines," said she, "which Dr. D. quoted, in his sermon on New Year's Day, about submission to God?"

"I have them in my porte-mounaie: he copied them for me, I was so much struck with them. He said he quoted them from memory,

but thought they were nearly right. Please
take the reins a moment, and I will read
them.

> ' With patience, then, the course of duty run:
> God never does, nor suffers to be done,
> But thou wouldst do thyself, couldst thou but see
> The end of all events as well as he.'"

"Oh!" said she, giving back the reins, "I
feel so safe when you are driving; and that
would do, by the way, to moralize upon. But
the thoughts in those lines have done more to
sustain me, or at least to keep my mind
quiet, than any uninspired words."

"No doubt it is literally true," said I, "that,
if we could have seen all which God saw, we
should have said, 'How desirable it is that
Agnes should die now!' We never would
have taken the responsibility of judging, however; and therefore it is well that there is One
who can, and who is willing to do so, and does
not spare for our crying."

"What are some of the reasons," said she,
"which you can imagine why it was best?"

"Oh! she might have had the seeds of disease in her, which would have made her life a burden," I replied.

"Or she might have proved a great trial to us in some way," she added.

"Perhaps," said I, "God wishes to prepare us to do great good in the world, and this is the preparative. If God seeks to fill us with himself, if he desires our love, what an honor it is, and what a privilege it is, to receive him even by displacing the dearest object."

"Why, there comes a hearse," said she; and true, we were about to meet a funeral.

The hearse proved to be some way in advance of the carriages, and was empty; the burial had taken place; the friends were returning.

I brought my horse to a walk; and, as the first carriage drove by, a lady in the deepest mourning had her face in her handkerchief, and was bowed half-way down, as in violent weeping, while the gentleman at her side, his hat off, leaned his head back, his face in like

manner covered, and he abandoned to grief.
Two sweet children, a boy and girl, were on
the front seat, the curtains rolled up, watching
the wet gravel which the wheels threw off.
We hardly noticed the other carriages.

"There," said I, "is grief, which perhaps
they would be willing to exchange for ours."

"I hope," said she, "that they have some
of the consolations which we possess. What
do people in such troubles as these do without
God?"

"Oh, they try and make the best of it," said
I; "they go into company, get relief in business or pleasures, and strive to outlive it; or
they become melancholy and useless. But
how much better it is to say, 'Show me
wherefore thou contendest with me;' and be
more anxious to know what God intends
and expects, than why the affliction happened."

"The greatest trial I have had," said she,
"in this affliction, is, to think that God is
angry with me for my sins, and is dealing
with me in wrath."

"Do you feel so?" said I, "for I am almost glad if you do, because I can tell you something which greatly helped me. I told Dr. D. when he called, the day that Agnes died, that my greatest trouble was, that God was angry with me for some particular sin, or for all my sins."

"What did he say to you?" said she.

"He said that he once preached a sermon on that very point. 'Behavior in trouble' was the subject, and he took this view of it: 'Admit the worst; you have been a great sinner in some particular; now God is dealing with you for it.

"'What will you do? Flee from him? be shy of him? feel angry and stubborn? No, but thank him that he is willing to take you in hand. Brambles,' he said, 'do not get pruned; vines are cut and thinned out.' Then he took your little Bible, which lay near, and read three beautiful passages, and turned down the leaves for me.

"One was this: 'Surely it is meet to be

said unto God, I have borne chastisement, I
will not offend any more.'

"This, he said, is Christian meekness; hum-
bling one's self under the mighty hand of
God; and it is our first duty."

"I saw those leaves turned down," said she,
"but what were the other passages?"

"The next, he said, tells us how God feels
towards us when he afflicts us, and we humble
ourselves: 'I have surely heard Ephraim bemoaning himself thus: Thou hast chastised
me, and I was chastised, as a bullock unaccus-
tomed to the yoke; turn thou me, and I shall
be turned; for thou art the Lord my God.'

'Then God speaks: 'Is Ephraim my dear
son? is he a pleasant child? for, since I spake
against him, I do earnestly remember him
still; therefore my bowels are troubled for
him; I will surely have mercy upon him,
saith the Lord.'"

Turning to witness her smile of gratification
at such words, I saw her face with tear after
tear coursing down upon it.

But how strangely mixed up are pathos and innocent mirth, in all that is natural, and in ways, too, which art cannot imitate without seeming unnatural. The horse, failing to discriminate between some sound which I made with my lips, and a chirrup, started off at a good round trot. This left a little less shading to our thoughts.

"You would not wish to stop at the cemetery," I said, "on our way home."

"Oh, no, not to-day," she replied : "it would only excite needless grief. Some pleasant morning we will ride out there."

"Why do you say the morning," I asked, "rather than the afternoon?"

"I like to take a bright sunny morning to visit a new grave," she said. "It helps me bear it better. The shadows and the approach of evening make me gloomy, and we ought not to expose ourselves to temptations in our trials. God helps those that help themselves. When months are passed, I like the afternoon."

"How many good thoughts you give me," said I, "besides cheering my spirits."

"I am glad if I do," said she; "but please go slower." The horse seemed to be in sympathy again with our pleasurable feelings, quickening his pace, and soon bringing us safely to our door.

CHAPTER V.

As we sat at breakfast the next morning, I remarked to my wife that I felt less pain with regard to that little key. I had been made to feel, as never before, that God's claim and his right to the child take precedence of ours; that the consecration of our children to him is eminently a duty as well as a privilege; and that our principles and feelings in habitually performing the duty, ought to have a controlling influence with us, if God sees fit to take our children away. One pleasant effect of these views was to make me feel that the death of our child was not in the main a loss, a total loss, as I had regarded it; but that, being a part of God's great purposes, her death would appear, at some time when it

45

would be as desirable to be happy as now, the
means of some great good.

So, instead of contriving where to place and
keep the key of the little coffin, I found my
self employed in asking, What good uses shall
I derive from it? and this led to the following
conversation, in one of our afternoon drives.

"You must give me that little key," said
my wife, in one of these excursions.

"Can you keep it better than I, or with
less risk of its disturbing your feelings?" I
inquired.

"You must gratify me in this thing," said
she, "without much inquiry. I will promise
to keep it safely, and make it as useful as I
can."

"Well," said I, "let us go to the little grave
together, some day, and take the key with us.
I should like to see how we shall feel there, in
view of our affliction, compared with our feelings at the burial."

A few months had elapsed since that event,
the weather had become fine, and so we agreed

one evening that we would spend the next morning at the cemetery.

What strange coincidences with the events of the day there sometimes are in our casual selection of passages of Scripture in our morning devotions! That morning, I opened my Bible with my thoughts full of our expected visit, and, for a moment or two, hardly looked upon the page; but, on beginning to read, the first words which met my eyes were these: "And said, Where have ye laid him? They say unto him, Lord, come and see."

It is as wrong to shape our conduct by passages of Scripture casually met with, as it is to follow dreams, or to trust in coincidences of any kind. Sad mistakes are often made by interpreting such coincidences in favor of our wishes. At the same time, we may receive wholesome instruction even from dreams, and coincidences ought to make us pause and reflect, so giving to sound judgment and discretion better opportunities for reflection. The occurrence of this passage, that morning, involving no question of duty, certainly was the occasion of no harm, if it made me reflect how the Holy Spirit, who indited the Bible, is pleased at times to be with us when we read it, and apply it to our circumstances. It is wrong to look upon passages of Scripture as omens, but we may derive comfort and instruction from them at pleasure. This passage made me think that Jesus feels an interest in the graves of our children and friends; that he looks down and watches all our dust, if we sleep in Jesus; and therefore I felt that he would accompany us to the grave of our child.

As my wife was about to take her seat in the carriage, and was putting on her gloves in the parlor, I asked, —

"What passage of Scripture do you think I have just seen which is applicable to you?"

Please tell me," said she, without lifting her eyes.

"'She goeth unto the grave to weep there.'"

After a moment's pause, she replied, "Mary

little knew what a scene she was going to witness there. Perhaps her Friend will go with us."

"I have invited Him," said I. "'Lord, come and see.'"

"And so," said I, as we drove along, "we are going to the grave in company with the Resurrection and the Life. What a privilege to have a grave, if it secures for us the special presence of Jesus!"

"I was struck with the remark, in the sermon last Sabbath," said she, "that, of the two who went to heaven without dying, God's own Son was not one of them."

"But here we are," said I, "at the stopping-place nearest to the path."

We walked along over ground where no foot seemed lately to have trodden on the numerous ant-hills where the busy little emmets were at work. We spoke of superior beings compassionating us, as we did these little creatures. We stepped over and among them as well as we could; for we had feelings

4

of tenderness toward every thing. A robin
ran across our path, with his head up, and a
worm dangling from his bill. The long
branches of the larch-trees bowed quietly under the pressure of a pleasant morning wind.
The stones, with their inscriptions, showing
their manifold histories of sorrow, seemed to
speak to us like people on a wreck saying to
some more impassioned sufferer, Think, too, of
us! Our hearts beat hard, we had to summon
new strength, as we caught the first sight of
the dear little mound. We leaned on the
fence, and wept, apart.

"But," said I, holding up the steps of my
companion, as we came nearer, "I cannot
think of her as here. Have you not put
away her little cloak, and other things of hers,
in the camphor trunk?"

"Yes," said she; "why do you ask?"

"Because," said I,

> "'Graves are but beds where flesh till morning sleeps,
> Or chests, where God awhile our garments keeps.'

" There will be a time when this will cease
to be an affliction. We shall see at last that
it was one of those 'all things' which work
together for good to them that love God."

" I try hard," she said, " to forget myself
and my affliction, and to consider how I may
best please God, and honor him in my trial.
I do not wish to be comforted, but to be useful; to be made better."

" That is the truest comfort also," said I.

" We are very insignificant things," said she,
" and our happiness or suffering ought not to
absorb our thoughts; but, how shall Christ be
magnified in us, by life or by death?"

" What an object," said I, " that is to live
for! How ennobling; and how small does
selfish sorrow appear!"

" We are flesh and blood," said she, " and
must weep and suffer under our trials."

" It would be unnatural if we did not," I
replied. " God expects us to cry when he
binds us. I went to see your friend L., you
know, after her husband was brought home

dead. A good woman came to meet me at the door, and said, 'Oh, Mr. M., you know what sorrow is; do come up and try to stop L.'s crying; she has been taking on so for six or eight hours.' L. heard this, as we entered the room. 'I cannot help it,' said she. 'Oh, Mr. M., what shall I do?' 'Cry as much as you please, dear L.,' said I: 'it will be a relief to you. Do not try to check it. I am glad to see that you can cry. David's Psalms are, many of them, nothing but spells of crying. Jesus groaned in spirit twice, as he went to the grave of Lazarus. I am sure you have enough to cry about.'"

"What effect did it have upon her?" asked my wife.

"At first," said I, "she wept as when a cloud bursts. I sat still a few moments, knowing it was only the reaction from her long effort to control her feelings. At length she grew calm; and, when I left her, she said, 'Well, I do feel that underneath are the everlasting arms.'"

"Oh !" said my wife, "what a world of sorrow, and to do good in, this is ; and I feel as though I wanted to go home and find out every afflicted heart, and be kind to it. Did you bring the little key with you?"

I produced it. How much my feelings had been mitigated since I drew it from my pocket the evening after the funeral! We looked at it with composure. He who turneth the shadow of death into the morning, and maketh the day dark with night, had been gracious to me. "I look upon that key," said Agnes, "as a sort of ordinance, a symbol; it represents a world of thought and feeling."

"That is a good idea," said I, "and let us improve upon it. I begin to think, that, when I see this little key hereafter, it will be with me as it is said of Hannah, 'Her countenance was no more sad.' I mean to make a good use of the little key. I should love to join with you, some evening, and put down in a little book our thoughts and feelings in connection with it. We shall read it, hereafter, with great satisfaction."

"You will forgive me," said I, "for not having told you that this is not my first visit here since the funeral. I have been here several times, but I did not wish to try your feelings by alluding to it. I came out here once when there were two feet of snow in this lot. This little grave was hidden."

"Oh, how beautiful and sad that must have looked!" she said.

"It was the first time that I came, after the funeral. I was glad not to see the little grave. I knew it was there, safe, beneath that beautiful mantle."

"What passages of Scripture did it make you think of?" she inquired: "you are so apt to see meanings in them which I do not."

I said to her, "I thought of this: 'He shall cover thee with his feathers, and under his wings shalt thou trust.' I felt that the snow was a great white wing spread over Agnes. The snow was wreathed around this silver-leaved maple, like a calla-lily around its pistil. How white and pure it was!—

> ' The fanned snow
> That's bolted by the northern blast thrice o'er.'

"I could not help weeping as I looked on those exquisitely beautiful curves of the snow, and I thought that the God who wrought such things would not, could not, deal with those who love him otherwise than in love and wisdom."

"I wish that I had seen it," said she.

"You could not have waded here," I replied. "And now here the grass is green, and the sods are putting out fresh spires on the mound. These changes are but ' the varied God. The rolling year is full of Thee.' Summer, autumn, winter, spring, will come in their turn and visit this little grave. God has a treasure here, which he is keeping for a great purpose.

"Last week, I was here again. This one thought absorbed me: The will of God is

better than child, or any other possession.
Had it been referred to me whether Agnes
should be restored to life, I would on no account have decided the question, but would
have referred it back again.   I feel so still.

"Let me read you some lines which I wrote
here last week, and then we will go : —

AT MY CHILD'S GRAVE.

Beneath this new-made mound
   An infant lies;
She cannot hear a sound :
   Closed are her eyes.
Her little form is mouldering back to clay :
With small and great she waits the judgment day.

God's watchful eye beheld
   This sparrow fall;
By him an infant's hairs
   Are numbered all.
God! in thy dreadful majesty, how mild!
O Christ! the Father, with thee, loves a little child.

She on her wondrous way
   Still looks behind,
And light still breaks all day
   Over her mind.

At the last trump she'll come with angel size
Down to this grave to watch the body rise.

> What shall the body be ? —
> > Now, like a grain,
> It dies, to bring forth fruit
> > And live again.
> This little seed shall yield a shock of corn;
> Out from this grave a form like Christ's shall greet the soul's
> > return.

"I must talk with you," she said, "about the doctrine in the last stanzas, as we are riding home."

"Last March," said I, "it did not seem possible that I could ever go away from this little grave with so much peace. I feel that we have left Agnes in heaven, rather than in the grave."

"Now please tell me," said she, "what makes you think that children do not remain children in heaven, as so many think that they do."

"It strikes me," said I, "as a very earthly idea that children are to be kept forever in infancy and childhood in heaven, as though we should need their childhood there to make us happy, as it does here. And why are we to suppose that the mind of a child will not expand in heaven, as well as here? Besides, it seems like doing them a wrong, to keep them in a childish condition forever."

"Oh! I cannot think so," said she. "To be a happy child in heaven forever, I think must be as real bliss as to be a full-grown mind. How children in heaven must be loved! How interesting they must be to angels! What exquisite pleasure a child has! I feel less and less the power of knowledge to make us happy. 'He that increaseth knowledge increaseth sorrow.' Your doctrine may be true for other reasons, but not, I think, because it will be any wrong to a child to keep it a child."

"I suppose you feel," said I, "that you would as soon be a member of a flower-garden as of a forest."

"Certainly: how much more pleasure I get

from a calla-lily than from a buttonwood," said she cheerfully. "But that is hardly fair," she continued. "We cannot properly compare flowers and trees, and give the preference to one over the other. Each has its place and use. Now, I feel that children are to heaven what flowers and birds are to nature here; and I want to have them remain so."

"That is woman's theology," said I. "You wish to find dear little Agnes a sweet little child, twenty or forty years hence, when you enter heaven."

"I love to think so," said she.

"It is a hard task," said I, "to argue against a mother, with so much on her side that is beautiful and touching, and especially when I know so little about it, after all"

"Then, perhaps," said she, "you had better be diffident, and not say much till you know more. I think you will have the mothers against you."

"Then I should beat a retreat, certainly," said I, "and go into camp; for I should hate to fulfil what Milton says about a woman reasoning with men : —

> ' In argument with men, a woman ever
> Goes by the worse, whatever be her cause.' "

"We should refute that in this case," said she, "as in many other instances, especially since we all know so little about the subject, for we should be hard pushed on either side to prove what we suppose. But I presume that it is the general belief, is it not, that the soul develops in heaven, as on earth ?"

"Analogy seems to favor it," said I, "certainly; but some people seem to think that we are to be re-constituted into families, in heaven, and that parents will gather their children about them, and have what they call happy homes. Therefore they like the thought of infants and young children remaining such.

"But," said I, "a father and mother, whose children grew up and left them, would have a solitary home, unless their children should all return ; but I certainly should not consent to your leaving me to live with your father and mother. More than this, would you rather have Agnes for a beautiful little plaything, or see her developed into a perfect form, and all her powers and faculties in full bloom, capable of appreciating every thing ? Parents are willing, here, to send their children away from them to school, as a duty they owe their children."

"That is because they will, of necessity, grow up, and therefore must be educated," said she.

" But no judicious parent, apart from this," said I, "would prefer to keep a child in a juvenile state, for the parent's own pleasure, rather than cultivate and inform its mind. Growth is probably the law of heaven, as of earth, — growth without decay."

"But what a loss it will be," she replied, " when all the children from earth are grown up in heaven ! I dread to think, for instance, that the time will come when the youngest person whom I shall see from earth will be a few thousand years old."

" 'It doth not yet appear what we shall be,' " said I. "All that we can say is, 'Thou hast created all things, and for thy pleasure they are and were created.' In God's own way we shall each fulfil some part in his great empire and plan; but growth is his plan."

"Well," said she, "we will take the little key, and sit down and contrive what to do with it, and how it shall do us good, and do good by us."

CHAPTER VI.

INSTRUCTIONS AND COMFORT FROM THE KEY.

It had rained very hard all day, a few weeks after this, when, as we sat at tea, Agnes said, —

"No one will come in this evening, and now let us have that conversation about the key."

It was soon brought down from her private drawer, in a tortoise-shell card-case, where she had kept it for some time. I had writing materials before me, and a memorandum book, which I proceeded to dedicate to its use, by writing these words on the first page : "The Key of a Little Coffin."

"Now," said I, "let us proceed somewhat after this method: I will name some use, or reflection, or purpose, suggested by the little

thing ; and when we have discussed it, I will
write it down here. Then it shall be your
turn to propose a sentiment."

"I fear," said she, "that you will have to
furnish most of the thoughts. But, if you will
begin, I will do my best. When we read it
over, we will recollect that it did not sound so
much like speeches when we talked, as I fear
it will from the book."

Husband. "One thing, then, which I love
to think of in connection with the little key,
is this : It can never be used for this purpose
again.

"I feel so glad that this is not a sorrow
which is in anticipation. We have passed
through the cloud, and through the sea, and
the waters themselves have been a wall to us
on either side, the affliction itself defending
us from many temptations, and constituting a
hiding-place for us. I have been instructed,
and, I trust, made better; but I am so glad
that I am not to pass through this trial again.
It is finished, and God has given us this key,

as it were, with those sacred words. I will record this, therefore, for a beginning. Will you give me a thought?"

Wife. "It is an emblem and pledge of re-opening. We use keys not merely to lock up. You seem to have regarded this key as a seal upon the stone. This is true, but let us also think of it as an emblem and a pledge of re-admission to her. She is ours still. She may have ten thousand instructors in heaven, but we are her parents. It seems to me a great honor to be a parent of a redeemed soul. How much nearer this brings us to a likeness with God than angels approach! You asked me, as we came from the funeral, whether I regretted all the sickness and sorrow which Agnes cost. To have a child in heaven is worth all that a parent can suffer. And now, the keenness of affliction having passed by, this key will seem to us like a hope which is laid up for us in heaven."

Husband. "This suggests a thought to me. The little key is a token of possession. She

5

is our precious child. Her past history, the
memory of her, the happiness she afforded us,
the love to each other of which she was the
occasion, the beautiful, hallowed thoughts
which we shall continue to have about her,
are a possession which no one can take from
us. She was God's gift, and she is ours still.
He has placed her away for a season, but has
given us the key, and it will make us feel
that we have a child in heaven. When
people say to us, ' Have you children?' we
shall answer, ' Yes, and one is in heaven.' "

Wife. "It will open a way for us to sorrowing hearts. How much good we may
now do in comforting and instructing others.
No one knows what this affliction is till they
have experienced it. I used to think I knew
all about it, while condoling with bereaved
mothers; but now I see my mistake. How
easy it seemed then to be reconciled, by thinking that God did it, and that the child was
better off, or a great many such true and
good things; but now I see that one may

have every consolation, and still the affliction
continue. I used to think otherwise. Now
I see that one who loses an arm may have all
Christian consolations; and yet, when he is
reminded every few moments that he has but
one arm, it is no less a calamity than though
he had no consolation, only he can bear it
better."

Husband. "I must read you a passage
from Shakspeare, if you will excuse me a
moment to bring the book from the library.

"The subject seems to be, ' Counsel of no
weight in misery.'

'I pray thee cease thy counsel,
  Which falls into mine ears as profitless
  As water in a sieve; give me not counsel,
  Nor let no comforter delight mine ear,
  But such a one whose wrongs do suit with mine.
  Bring me a father that so loved his child,
  Whose joy of her is so o'erwhelmed like mine,
  And bid him speak of patience,
  Measure his woe the length and breadth of mine,
  And let it answer every strain for strain;
  As thus for thus, and such a grief for such.
  If such a one will smile, and stroke his beard,

Cry, sorrow, wag! and hem, when he should **groan**
Patch grief with proverbs, make misfortune **drunk**
With candle wasters, — bring him yet to me,
And I of him will gather patience.
But there is no such man. For, brother, men
Can counsel, and speak comfort to that grief
Which they themselves not feel; but, tasting **it,**
Their counsel turns to passion, which before
Would give preceptial medicine to rage,
Fetter strong madness in a silken thread,
Charm ache with air, and agony with **words.**
No, no; 'tis all men's office to speak patience
To those that wring under the load of sorrow:
But no man's virtue, nor sufficiency,
To be so moral, when he shall endure
The like himself; therefore give me no counsel :
My griefs cry louder than advertisement.'" *

Wife. "Some people seem fond of preaching to others in trouble; but a little sympathy, a drawing near to one, a kind word, or
look, or token of remembrance, how it holds
us up ! It is not so much what is said, as
the manner, indicating the disposition, and
making you feel that you are not forsaken."

Husband. "Why do you suppose the

* Much Ado about Nothing, Act. V.

Saviour took those three men with him when he was going into Gethsemane? He left them at the entrance."

Wife. "I suppose he loved to feel that he had friends near. How natural this is!"

Husband. "And what a beautiful idea it gives us of the human sympathies of Jesus, touched with the feeling of our infirmities!"

Wife. "But there is one way of showing sympathy which I desire to avoid, for I suffered from it more than I can tell. Calls on a bereaved person are, for the most part, agonizing, unless there be great intimacy between the parties; in other cases, there is a questioning, and a moralizing, and a probing into all the secret, painful parts of the affliction, and a rehearsing of afflictions which the visitor herself had passed through, which does much to keep the wound from healing over. I am resolved that, unless I am on very intimate terms, or in a peculiar relation to a bereaved person, I will express my sympathy merely by some message, or little gift, or act of remembrance, and not by being one of twenty or thirty people to make the poor sufferer go over the bitter tale again and again, or to make her sit and endure a stiff, ceremonious visit."

Husband. "Some people like, and even expect, such things. To me it is almost so many bereavements. But I had almost forgotten one more thought, which the little key has suggested. It is given to us by Him who has the keys of death. This is one of them. Oh, how many such keys he has! He shutteth and no man openeth. Did we not know that he loves us, should we not feel that he mocked us, and that for an egg he had given us a scorpion? 'Take this key,' he seems to say. 'I have taken Agnes away from you. No one will question my right to do so. She was mine before she was yours, and after she became yours. The number of her months was with me. Take this key. Keep it as a mark of my sovereignty, and a badge of your unquestioning submission.' Can you assent to this, my love, and shall I write it down?"

Wife. "I cannot be stationary in my love to God in times of affliction. I must part with him, or love him more than ever. I choose the latter. This is a new unfolding of his character to us. We cannot, therefore, feel toward God precisely as we did before. Now, if I question his perfect rectitude and love, I become an atheist; instead of this, I will love him more than ever, in proportion as he reveals himself, even though it be in affliction. — Are you waiting for me to propose a thought? One thing I wish that this little key would do for me. It must lock up unpleasant recollections."

Husband. "May I ask, before they are locked up, that you will let me know some of them?"

Wife. "We have spoken of them, you know, several times. I find myself dwelling on second causes, and making myself needlessly unhappy. If we had only sent for the

physician on the first day that Agnes was sick,
instead of letting our kind friend give her
that medicine! It weakened her, and made
her less able to bear the disease, which otherwise she might have thrown off. But oh, that
thoughtless woman, putting sheets on her crib
which had just come from ironing without being aired! The doctor said that it did harm.
Besides, I never felt sure that, the night before
Agnes died, the girl did not give her the
wrong medicine.

"The doctor looked surprised when he saw
that the new phial, which he ordered the evening before, had not been used the next morning. Phœbe says she gave her no medicine,
I shall always feel that she gave her those
hurtful drops, by mistake. But then, I say,
why dwell on these things? We did the best
that we knew how to do at the time. If the
thing itself was appointed to happen, so were
the means to produce it; and so let all these
things go into the grave. Only we shall learn
wisdom by experience."

Husband. " I will gladly change this topic, and say : I will not part with this key, and yet I cheerfully give my child to God.

" I heard some one say, in a sermon, that an English lady had a fine flower on a very rare plant, with which she was so enraptured that she wished the queen might have it; and, being on suitable terms with the sovereign, she had it conveyed to her. I think it is not that God had the right to my child, that makes me submissive : I love him, and, if he wishes for my child, he shall have her, and me, too. But no money, no persuasions, could get this key from me."

Wife. " Do let me name one thing more, lest I forget it, — if you had finished. The little key is a symbol of individuality and separateness. Sometimes I lose Agnes in a great crowd of children in heaven. Our min· ister said, that probably more have gone to heaven in childhood, than in any other period of life. ' Where is our little girl ?' I find my-self saying. She is not lost in the crowd. Spe·

cial assignments have been made with regard
to her; she is in the hands of those, who, if I
could see them, would make me feel perfectly
happy in leaving her with them. Her grave
is a separate one. No other grave on earth
can be confounded with it in our thoughts.
This is the key to nothing but her little coffin.
And now is there not as much individuality
and separateness in the love and care of God
for her?"

Husband. "Christ said of little ones,
'That in heaven their angels do always behold the face of my Father which is in
heaven.'"

Wife. "Pray, what does that mean? for I
never understood it."

Husband. "It means, I have been told,
that angels who minister to these little ones
are not inferior beings, but 'presence angels;'
they are deemed worthy of the chiefest care,
and are in charge of those who can say, as
the angel said to Mary, 'I am Gabriel, that
stand in the presence of God.'

"Your thought about individuality and separateness makes me think of this: Suppose that every little coffin had a little key, trimmed with white ribbon, and that they should all be hung up in our sight. What a wilderness of them there would be! We should be unwilling to attach undue importance to our little treasure; we should say, Tens of thousands have suffered all that we have suffered; and, at the same time, God has as distinct a knowledge of our loss, and of our dear child, as though she were the only object of his care. Let me say one thing more; I believe it is my turn: I am admitted by this key to companionship with all who have children in heaven.

"Now I do feel, after all, that there is some honor and privilege in being selected by Christ to contribute an infant soul to his mediatorial crown. I am glad that I had a flower in my garden so precious that the Lord of all wished to transplant it for me to his own special care and love. A peasant is pleased when a nobleman or his lady stops at his gate and asks for a slip from some beautiful plant. I look upon a family where there are many children, and say to myself, 'You have no dear little representative of your number in heaven. You, parents, have never had the privilege of sending a sweet envoy to the court of God. You would not choose to send one, nor would we choose it for you. But, had God seen fit to take some little child of yours to himself, I feel that you would, in time, be glad, and at death your meeting with it would have a rapture which would make you bless God that he took away your little one to enhance your joy.' Now, this little key says to us, 'You belong to that favored band who, at their coming, will receive their own with usury.' The key is a decoration, a badge of membership. I am glad to belong to such a communion, even at such a cost. I have a child at court. She is a maid of honor. O Saviour! we thank thee for numbering us with those who are counted worthy of this."

Wife. " It is time to finish, for the pres·
ent, I suppose ; but one more thought occurs
to me, and, as you began, I will conclude :
May I take this key with me, if I go astray ?

" How God can punish us ! What arrows
he has in his quiver ! How he knows where
to strike ! The little key says to us : 'Go
thy way, sin no more, lest a worse thing
happen unto thee.' Sad is it to think that in
the course of time we may depart from
God, that some worldly influences may take
our hearts away from Christ; we may become lovers of pleasure ; temptations,
through prosperity, may ensnare both of us ;
we know not what we are capable of; affliction has no power in itself to keep us in the
path of duty. If we ever wander, may a
sudden, accidental sight of this little key
remind us how perishable are earthly joys,
how fading its honors, how insecure its pos-
sessions, how entirely God can dispose of us ;
and, moreover, that we were never so safe,
and never happier, than when we were in af

fliction. Let us pray to God that he will use
this little key to lock up our way, if we
should seem to wander from him. I really
feel afraid to come out of trouble. A season
of affliction is freed from many a snare.
What was it that Bunyan's pilgrims said
when they came into the Valley of Humilia-
tion, and fell down and kissed the flowers of
the place? It was this, I think : —

'He that is down needs fear no fall,
   He that is low, no pride;
He that is humble ever shall
   Have God to be his guide.' "

Husband. " When we have felt and said
all that is right and proper, the affliction re-
mains. It was intended as an affliction, and,
as one said, 'This is a lamentation, and shall
be for a lamentation.' Every now and then
I find myself thinking how old Agnes would
have been at the present time. There is no
such relaxation to a weary man as a little
child. How often I have hastened home

from business meetings, just for the sake of taking that little child into my arms and forgetting every thing in watching it. A parent, in the play, says of a little child, —

> ' He's all my exercise, my mirth, my matter,
>   And, with his varying childness, cures
>   Thoughts that would thick my blood.' "

Wife. "O, what a loss it is! But ' the Lord gave, and the Lord hath taken away, blessed be the name of the Lord.' "

Husband. "Let us agree that to-morrow we will begin and see what good we can do, under the influence of what we have experienced."

Wife. "I have marked out several plans, and at some future time we will discuss them."

CHAPTER VII.

ANNIVERSARIES OF BEREAVEMENTS.

THE anniversary of Agnes' death and funeral arrived. We passed through the first of these sustained by the thought that the burial had not transpired, thus deceiving ourselves with one of those stratagems in which the afflicted are only less ingenious than the insane. And when the anniversary of the funeral came, I said to myself, 'She was not buried till Friday, — this is the 10th, the same day of the month, indeed, but it is not Friday.' When the next day came, we said, 'This is not the day; she was not buried on the 11th, but yesterday was the true anniversary.' Such was my weakness.

We had looked forward to these days with sad apprehensions, and wished that they were past. Still, we endeavored to go through them submitting to the mighty Hand that appoints times and seasons, and does not change the order of Nature for any of his creatures. We knew that we should suffer, and we regarded it as an appointed part of our trial.

So we repaired to the room where the dear child died, and, as the hour arrived, never to be forgotten, we prayed together, and, amidst tears and interrupted utterances, we acknowledged the perfect right which God had to bereave us; confessed that any thing short of endless misery was less than our deserts; rejoiced that we had a child in heaven, one treasure where no thief approacheth; gave thanks for the support afforded us in our trial, and especially that it had made us in any degree useful to others; and we prayed earnestly, and above all things, that God would fulfil his purposes in this affliction, whatever they might be.

That evening I brought from the post-office a letter to my wife, from her most intimate

6

and endeared female friend, who had gone to a distant part of the world with her husband, to reside for several years. The letter proved to be the lady's journal for several months, and it was dated a year ago and upon the day that Agnes died. She began by saying: " My dearest Agnes, I know not why it is, but I feel an irrepressible impulse to begin a history for your entertainment. So I date my long letter forthwith, but oh, what events may betide us before this reaches you!" The letter was a most entertaining account of a lady's experience and observations in a city on the other side of the globe, interspersed with narratives of short voyages and travels. Of course, it furnished food for thought and conversation till late that night, bringing tears of joy at some girlish reminiscences of school days, and other tears at the congratulations which it bore on hearing of the birth of our child.

"Dated," said my wife, "the day that Agnes died, and received on the next anniversary : how interesting!"

"I suppose," said I, "some people would wonder at us; but I choose, at the risk of being wrong, to see and acknowledge a good, kind Hand in such coincidences. I am not unwilling to believe that the all-seeing God, looking at once on us and on your friend the other side of the globe, devised this coincidence, and has brought it about for our comfort. 'He stayeth his rough wind in the day of his east wind.' 'But I am poor and needy, yet the Lord thinketh upon me.'"

"What an idea it gives us," said she, "of the omnipresence of God!"

"And how it illustrates," I observed, "the ease with which God plans different events far asunder in time and space, and brings them together, matched and finished, in his appointed time. Just think of what it was necessary for Him to do, on the waves and with the winds, and by means of the numerous conveyances and the scores of men who had charge of them, and of the mails, if it were his purpose to bring that letter to our door, not yesterday, nor to-morrow, but on this anniversary."

"If he did all this for our little comfort," said she, " it makes me say, as the people did of Jesus at the grave of Lazarus, ' Could not this man, which opened the eyes of the blind, have caused that even this man should not have died ?' Surely, he could have spared Agnes to us, and he was willing to do so, but his reluctance to make us suffer was over-ruled by higher considerations. This letter, coming to-night, persuades me to feel, more than ever, that God is as kind and good in our trials as in our blessings, if we love him."

But the anniversary of the burial arrived, — the day of the week, that Friday, — and we wept apart much of the time, and when we were together, we each made an effort, now and then, to break the silence, for we were so troubled that we could not speak. After tea, I went to the post-office, with the intention of returning soon and spending the evening at home.

Who would have thought that I could stay away till ten o'clock that night?

I returned at that hour, having sent word home to that effect, and found my wife waiting for me in the parlor. A book which she had been reading lay on the table before her, and with it her handkerchief, which, as I passed round, I involuntarily took up to catch from it a very rare perfume, which a friend from Malabar had lately given her. But underneath the handkerchief lay the tortoise-shell card-case.

"Oh, what have you been doing with this?" said I.

"Having some very profitable thoughts over it," she replied. "But come and tell me what has happened to you, for it must be something strange to have detained you all the evening."

I held the card-case in my hand, and no doubt I used some sign of endearment toward it, for I could not help exclaiming, "Oh, what a blessing is a peaceful death, an honored burial, an innocent grave!" I felt happy to see that little key.

"What makes you feel so happy?" said she. "Pray tell me where you have been, and what has happened to you."

"I have just come from the jail," said I.

In her endeavors to comfort those that mourn, my wife heard that a youth who had been tried for his life on a charge of murder, and was brought to our city jail for safer custody, was the son of a woman whom she had once or twice employed in household work. She had become intemperate, through domestic trouble, and the son had killed his companion at a gambling-table. He was now awaiting his execution. My wife had interested our minister, Dr. D., in the young man, so that, as soon as he was lodged in our jail, the clergyman sought and obtained permission to visit him.

The result of his visits was, that the youth gave signs of penitence, and had embraced the offers of pardon through the sufferings and death of Christ.

"On my way to the post-office," said I, " Dr. D. met me at his door, and told me that he was going to the cell, and asked me to go with him. I asked Mrs. D. to come and spend the evening with you, till I returned. I presume that company detained her.

" You know that to-morrow is the day fixed for the execution. Through the small holes over the doors of the cell, we saw here and there a face of one and another who had been aroused by the entrance of the jailer after dark. Michael, your poor boy, was sitting on the side of his cot-bedstead, in his shirt-sleeves, as we entered, when he shook hands with Dr. D., looking at the same time at me, and, as I could not but think, with the thought flashing through his mind whether I had come with any message of hope or relief.

" I saw a silver can on his rough table, and took it up, thinking that it looked familiar; and there was the inscription, ' Agnes : from her Grandmother.' He saw me looking at it,

and said that a kind lady had sent him some
broth in it. Did you send it in the can
purposely?"

"I was looking for something else," said
she, "and saw the can; and the contrast between Michael's mother and myself, as to our
children, struck me so, that I could not help
sending it as an acknowledgment of God's
mercy to me."

"As I held the can in my hands," said I,
"the same thought occurred to me, and I said
to myself, 'I will take the cup of salvation,
and call on the name of the Lord.' I told
Michael that I knew the lady, and this was a
sufficient introduction.

"Dr. D. began to talk with him about the
Lord Jesus Christ, and opened to him, as he
observed he had often done before, the great
truth of the gospel, free and full remission
of sins to every one who accepts and pleads
Jesus Christ, the Lamb of God, as the sacrifice
for sin. 'Michael,' said he, 'what could you
do now without an atoning Saviour, one that

has suffered for you? Your day of grace is nearly out; you cannot live to atone for your own sins, even if it were possible ever to do it. But the Son of God has answered all the demands of justice for you by bearing your sins in his own body on the tree. Man cannot justly pardon you; he cannot make any substitution for your punishment which would answer the ends of justice as your own death will do. But God can, as it respects all your sins, and now you are going to the bar of God before this time to-morrow, pleading, "Who is he that condemneth? It is Christ that died." '"

Wife. "How did Michael look? Was he crying?"

Husband. "I shall never forget his posture, his action, his emphasis, as, with his head on one side, his neck bare, and in his stockinged feet, he lifted up his head and said, —

"'Dr. D., I am such a sinner that nothing makes me feel safe only that God's own Son died for me. I was telling the turnkey, 'It's

all the same as God. He was God. I can't
puzzle it out, only I know he was God " — fum-
bling over his testament and reading John i.
1, — "And the Word was God." The fact is,'
said he, 'I am afraid I sent Dick Ross to
misery; he was as wicked a sinner as I am,
and that's as bad as can be; and now I
ought to go there, too; it seems as though I
couldn't get along, no how, without going
there, too; it's so just, you see, for I can't pay
for it no way nor no shape; it isn't worth the
first red cent, all I can ever do, and I made
up my mind to go and suffer, till you told
me how God could save me, Christ wanted
to save me, and Christ suffered what would
have been the same as hell for me. Now
you're sure, Doctor, that this is all so, I suppose — and this gentleman, does he think so,
too ? — My goodness,' said he, smiling, 'I
needn't ask, for I've had such feelings here,
that I didn't know what to make of 'em; only
it's too much; I don't know why He wants to
save me. He hadn't ought to save me, so to

speak, and I have told him so, but something
kept putting these words into my mind,
" won't cast 'em out, won't cast 'em out," " save
'em to the outmost," — and I set up and sung
that Methodist hymn, — oh, how I used to
sing it through my nose to mock the folks at
the Methodists', and I learnt it by mocking
'em, — so I set up and sung it last night as
loud as I could, and the people here all round
cried out to me not to make such a racket,
but go to sleep.'"

" And the prisoners heard them," said my
wife. " What was the hymn ? Why did you
not ask him to say it to you?"

" We did," said I.

" He folded his arms, and raised his eyes,
and sung, —

When I was sinking down, sinking down, sinking down,
When I was sinking down, sinking down;
Jesus resigned his crown, Jesus resigned his crown, Jesus
        resigned his crown,
    To save my soul.'

"In the third line, his hands were unfolded, and were lifted up with his eyes.

"'Now,' said he, 'that's as true as preaching; and if Christ wants to save me, I shall let him, and all I can do will be to praise him through all eternity. Oh, I wish I hadn't laughed at good folks so. But there, I'm to be saved; but if He hadn't died for me He couldn't have proved it to me, nor made me believe it. And if he hadn't have been God, nothing could have made me feel that there was any grounds to stand on. What touches God, you see, is dreadful, — it's beyond every thing, and if God did it, it covers every thing. Doctor,' said he, 'I ain't afraid to die; it's short: I'll fix my eyes on Christ, and feel that I'm going straight to him. Oh, poor Dick! he lived till morning, and they had a minister to him, and may be he's saved: how he'll shake hands and forgive me; but, if he isn't, must I be lost because he is? or hasn't Christ a right to pick out whom he's a mind to, all as bad as the rest, and save him for nothing?

What shall I do if he doesn't? Oh, he will, he will! "Of whom I'm chief:" no sir, beg your pardon, Michael Runy is that same; how they will look up to see me coming! "Why, there's Michael Runy, that murdered Ross!" Well, it'll teach 'em something they never knew before. Doctor,' said he, ' don't you never preach nothing but this: you tell people, as strong as you can, that God wants to save every mother's son of 'em. Step in among them men and boys that's smoking afore the bank every Saturday evening, and tell them about Michael Runy and Jesus Christ. There ain't one of 'em, if ye'll speak kind and affectionate like, but what'll hear you and thank you; and nothing else but talking to them about Jesus Christ will touch 'em.'

"He would have gone on all night with his wonderful flow of thought and words. I wished that I could have had all the divinity students in the land in that cell and corridor, to hear that dying man's lecture on the atonement, and his exhortation on preaching Christ.

"But Dr. D. said to him: 'Your mother told me, yesterday afternoon, Michael, that you wished to be baptized. Do you? I should like to do it for you if you wish.'

"'Yes, sir,' said Michael; 'I asked mother if she would be willing to come too, and she said, No, she wasn't good enough herself. Says she, "Mike, if I had only had you trained up in the ways of the Lord, you'd have never come to this." "Well, no matter," says I, "mother; don't take on so; only turn about yourself, and get religion, and look out for David and Madge, — they're young; and if you'll give up that cursed drinking, mother" — "I will," says she, "Mike, I haven't tasted no sperits sence the constable took you from dinner that day; and I won't. I had a bottle under the table, but I flung it away."'"

"Did you know," said my wife, "that he was once engaged to be married to a very respectable girl, a cousin of our cook?"

"He told us so," said I. "Dr. D. asked him why he wished to be baptized?"

"'Ruthy Dewire,' said he, 'that married the blacksmith's son down by the little bridge, used to company with me till she was con-verted, and when she saw she couldn't change me, she left off going with me. I went to see her taken into the Methodists'. She was the only one. She took her bonnet off, and kneeled down, and the minister read a little, and took her hand, and put his on her head. It was solemn, very solemn, 'specially when he said those words over her, "Father, Son, and Holy Ghost." I felt that them three were taking notice of Ruthy, she that used to go with me, and I couldn't understand why such solemn names were said over her. I asked her about it. She said it meant that she was given up to them to take care of her, and she was to mind what they said to her in the Bible. Ruthy seemed so holy after that, I should have broke off from her if she hadn't; it made me so solemn to look at her after that. But you can tell me, Doctor, more about what it means.'

"'In the first place,' said Dr. D., 'you must not feel that it will save your soul.' 'Oh, I don't,' said Michael; 'that's done; the Lord did that.' 'I am glad you feel so,' said Dr. D.; 'being baptized helps you feel that God and you make a covenant together; you give yourself up to him. He also gives you a seal of his being yours. You promise to renounce sin, as eating the bread and wine is a promise to love and obey Christ, and a help in doing it. Water cannot wash away sins, of course; it signifies our purpose to put them away. I wish your parents, Michael, had been good people, and that you had been godly while growing up, and that your parents had helped you put off sin and brought you up for God. But now you can turn to God and be accepted by him; for the promise is " Whosoever confesseth and forsaketh his sins shall find mercy."

"'And, while you thus put off sin, God promises to be your God, and he writes his

name upon you, and takes you to be his. Do
you understand all this, Michael ? '

" ' Every word of it, sir ; my grandmother
made me say the Bible and hymns to her
every Sunday night, in the old country, and
I guess she prayed for me ; and God has
skipped over my father and mother, and re-
members her prayers ; but, when we came
over here, father and mother fell out, and
father died, and mother got into a bad way.
Oh, do look after mother, won't you ? Tell her
how grandmother's talk all comes back to me,
and makes me see things quick, and understand them.' "

" Have you not sometimes noticed this,"
said my wife, — " a child of vicious parents
turning out remarkably well, or, like this
boy, becoming a Christian ; and, on inquiry,
found that some near ancestor of his had been
distinguished for piety ? But do not let me
interrupt you."

" ' Michael,' said Dr. D., ' do you truly re
7

pent of all your sins, and do you wish to put
away sin ?'

"*Michael.* 'I do, sir.'

"*Dr. D.* 'Do you believe on the Lord
Jesus Christ, the Saviour of sinners, and that
he came from heaven to suffer and die on the
cross for you ?'

"*Michael.* 'That I do, sir, surely.'

"*Dr. D.* 'Do you know, Michael, that in
those days the cross was their gallows, and
that the Son of God died, as you will die to-
morrow, only worse, but without sin ?'

"*Michael.* 'Oh, my soul, Doctor! I never
thought of that.'

"*Dr. D.* 'Yes: for it is written, "Cursed
is every one that hangeth on a tree." Christ
was "made a curse for us." Now, even poor
prisoners like you, who are going to the gallows, need not despair, for Jesus Christ, "whom
they slew and hanged on a tree," died for
them.'

"He dropped on his knees, and cried: 'O
Lord Jesus Christ! now I know it will not be

hard to die. Them nails, for me! and them thieves! and the thorns! and how they mocked him, and spit on him, and him the Son of God! Lord Jesus, I am another dying thief; Lord, remember me when thou comest in thy kingdom.'

"The turnkey moved round and looked out through the grated door, as though he heard a noise without, but I saw him draw his whole shirt-sleeve across his eyes, after he had turned away.

"Baptism was then administered, the jailer having provided means for a decent performance of the rite. Dr. D. read the account, in the Acts of the Apostles, of the jailer's baptism.

"It was now half-past nine. Michael had risen, and had been whispering to the turnkey, and then said, 'Doctor, could you possibly stay here all night?' The Doctor told him that he would stay with pleasure. I have just called at his house to inform his family. There are many worse things," said

I, "than having a little child taken from you to heaven. What a perfectly safe place it is!"

"Well," said my wife, "I am glad that you spent the evening so. It was as good for you as the letter the other evening was for me."

"Had it not been for the little key," said I, "probably you would not have been led to take the interest in Michael which has led to such good results. How much I thought of dear little Agnes while I was in the cell this evening! But tell me how you have spent the evening. I should have had no peace had I thought you were alone."

"I have been trying the power of unconditional submission to God, apart from all consolations," said she. "I am afraid of making terms with God. People used to comfort me by suggesting a great many good things in the way of consolation, but this is the only true comfort, I think: 'Thy will be done.' 'The cup which my heavenly Father hath given me, shall I not drink it?'"

"I think you are right," said I. "It is
delightful to let God see that you can trust
and love him, when you cannot understand
him. This looking out for compensation in
affliction is mercenary and selfish. It is good
to let the Most High do any thing with us,
and we be still and know that he is God.
Nothing touches us more than a patient, meek
spirit, and a cheerful behavior, in another,
when under reproof from us. It must make
God love one whom he has greatly afflicted
to see him cheerful in his sorrow, and hear
him praising God. Even in evil men, such
submission moves the compassion of God.
'Seest thou how Ahab humbleth himself
before me? I will not bring the evil in his
days.' Oh this unconditional submission to
God, as God! — it is the height of piety. I
try to go about my work in doing good to
others with more love to God than though
he had not taken Agnes from us. I wish to
show him that I love him better than I love
his gifts. How many things happen, like this

contrast of Michael's end, to help us in doing so!"

"I suppose," said she, "that it is right to accept of consolations and helps; only let the consolations be in the superstructure, and let the foundation of comfort be the will of God."

"I think you have it in the right order," said I; "but see how late it is."

After prayers, I took the tortoise-shell card-case with me to my private room. I stood where I did just a year ago, the evening after the funeral, with the little key in my hand. I thanked God that I had such a child in such a grave; and, in praying for Michael and his mother, I thought what a privilege it was to have that little key as the exponent of my affliction, instead of such memorials of her child as his mother would carry with her to the grave. In the morning "I awaked, and beheld, and my sleep was sweet unto me."

CHAPTER VIII.

BURIAL OF THE DROVER'S CHILD.

· WE attended the funeral of a little child, in whom my wife had become interested during its sickness. It was a noble boy of three years of age, who died of croup. Such beautiful golden hair, flowing over its face and into its bosom, I never saw. The features were not affected by any previous disease; all but the pale, icy look, which death brings with it, made you feel that the child was asleep.

The father was a drover. He was a stout, coarse-looking man, with a very large head, which he leaned back against the ceiling where he sat, rolling it to and fro, with his mouth open, the tears running down with no effort to conceal them or wipe them away;

and every now and then he would beat with
his head against the wall. The poor man
made me think of one of his own bullocks
drawn by a rope and windlass to the
slaughter. His wife was a small, delicate
woman, a Christian; but he was wholly neg-
lectful of religion and its ordinances.

I sat near him at the funeral, and wept
with him. No one could refrain. Being on
intimate terms, I asked him if I might go to
the grave with him.

" Oh ! do, sir," said his wife ; " I know he will
be so glad to have you. I try to comfort Mr.
Burke, but you know better how to do it."

" Go in our carriage," said he, " will you ? "

" Ask your wife to go with us," said she ;
" the ride will do her good."

So we found ourselves with them on our
way to the same cemetery where Agnes lay.

" A more beautiful sight," said I, " probably
was never beheld than your dear little boy in
his coffin. It makes me feel that the words
in a hymn by George Whitefield, whom you

have heard of, the great preacher. are some-times true :

> ‘ Ah, lovely appearance of death !
>   No sight upon earth is so fair;
> Not all the gay pageants that breathe
>   Can with a dead body compare.’

“ Your only child, too,” said I. “ Do you think that there is any God, Mr. Burke ?”

Mr. B. “ Well, I know there is.”

Mr. M. “ You know, too, that he did this.”

Mr. B. “ Of course. He does every thing.”

Mr. M. “ You cannot feel perfectly will-ing, I know, that he should do this; you would not be a natural father if you did.”

Mr. B. “ Oh ! ” said he, taking off his hat, and throwing his head back, convulsively, several times, “ I wish I was dead ; I don’t want to live. If that was the end of me, like an ox, I should be glad to be killed.”

Mr. M. “ My dear sir, you are going to

see the day when you will say that the death
of this dear little boy was the best thing
that ever happened to you. Only be patient
and try to be quiet."

Mr. B. " How can I ? " Then he began
to cry aloud.

It is dreadful to hear a man cry. The dis-
tressing, inarticulate, choked noises which he
made, set his wife into a violent weeping.;
but it was composing to listen to her grief
compared with his.

I thought of an expedient to divert his
mind. " Let me show you something which
will interest you," said I.

I took out the tortoise-shell card-case, and
waiting some little time to get his attention
fully, I said, —

" There is something in this which once
made me weep just as you do, Mr. Burke. I
have cried over it like a child. I do not
wonder at your crying, and I could hardly
believe once that I could see it now without
the same distress which I felt then, and which
you now feel."

"Do tell," said he; "I've no idea what it can be."

The little key was produced. I asked him to read the inscription on the ribbon.

Mr. B. "Well, I suppose you keep her things locked up, and this is the key of them."

Mr. M. "No, my dear sir, it is the key to her. She is locked up, and this did it. They are going to give you just such a key; I saw the undertaker put it in his pocket when he left the house."

"Oh! how can you keep it?" asked his wife; "I should think it would distract you every time you see it."

"I told my husband the same," said my wife, "when I found that he had brought it away from the grave. But we take great pleasure in it now."

Mrs. B. "I wish you would take ours and keep it for us."

Mr. M. "We will talk about it by and by. But only look out here " (for we were

within the cemetery), "and see how many
little stones there are over little graves.
Some parents have been here with their little
children before us, Mr. Burke."

Mr. B. "My stars! how thick they are!
Wife, just look out here : there are two,
three, five small graves in one lot. Do you
suppose they all belonged to the same people?"

Mr. M. "It is a vale of tears, Mr. B. If
all these parents who have lost children were
here, they would come and shake hands with
you, and say, 'Mr. Burke, we know what it
is ; don't be cast down; hope in God.'"

Mr. B. "I declare, I never felt that I
could have a moment's comfort; but I do
pity all these people so, who have buried so
many children! Dare say some of them
were as interesting as mine. But, oh! I can't
get over it. O George! dear little fellow,
must we leave you here in that awful grave?
Oh, if I hadn't been born!"

Mrs. B. "Don't, husband · I beg of you.

Other people have suffered just so, and got
over it. Here are Mr. M. and his wife, and
I'm sure it was as hard to lose their little
Agnes. See how they feel now. It's
because they are Christians; and if only you
were one, I shouldn't feel half so bad ; for,"
said she, " there's another parting with
George that'll be worse than this."

Mr. B. " Can't be worse than this, no
how; nothing can be worse than this."

Mr. M. " Oh, my dear sir! only think that
you must die and appear before God. Well,
perhaps little George comes to meet you, so
glad and happy, and says, ' Father, have you
really come ? Mother is here, — we're waiting for you.' But you are affrighted, and
find' you have no Saviour, and must go away.
How would you bear to be separated from
George then ? Now, you hope to meet him
again ; but then you will bid him farewell forever, and think of him and his mother in
heaven, and you shut out. Which is worse,
that, or this funeral ? "

He put his face on his hand, rested his
elbow in his other hand, looked out of the
carriage, and did not speak for a few minutes,
till finally he said, —

"All children go to heaven, I suppose?"

"I think they do," said I. "But they owe
it to Christ if they do. Should they grow up
here, they would grow up sinners, and therefore they need to be born of the Spirit, in
order to enter heaven; and this they receive,
we suppose, through Christ, who died for
them. Did you ever commune, Mrs. Burke?"

"Oh, no," said she, covering her face with
her handkerchief, and weeping. "Mr. Burke
could never be persuaded, and I did not wish
to go alone. He used to say he felt ashamed
to stand up before so many people; and, besides, he never saw any great use in it."

"I don't feel so now," said Mr. B.

"How would you do now?" inquired I.

"Why," replied he, "I would please my
wife. I see now what a comfort it would be
to her, though I do not see into it. I wish

we could do it at the grave, if I was good
enough."

"There is time yet," said I: "but soon 'there
is no work, nor device, nor knowledge, nor
wisdom, in the grave whither thou goest.'"

"Perhaps," said Mr. B., "he wouldn't have
been taken away from us if I had offered him
up, as wife called it, with prayer to God."

"Our little girl who died was offered up,"
said my wife. "That makes no difference."

"But, oh," said Mrs. Burke, "what a comfort it must be to you now! I had some spells
of crying over it."

"Oh, don't talk about that, wife," said Mr.
B.; "you know I wouldn't do the same now."

"I didn't mean to reproach you, my dear,"
said she, "I was only thinking aloud. You
are very kind to me, only we never thought
just alike, you know."

I said, "I cannot but hope that you will;
God may make this the greatest blessing to
both of you."

We had been winding slowly up hill and

down hill, stopping to let other carriages pass
on their return; and at length we came to a
remote part of the inclosure, a very humble
place in it, where Mr. Burke, at the request
of his wife, had, the day before, secured a very
cheap lot, which she said she wished to feel
was her own, and which she could visit and
plant with flowers.

"So Jesus slept," said I, as we stopped.

> " ' God's dying Son
> Passed through the grave and blessed the bed.'

"This is like the Saviour's burying-place,
'wherein never man before was laid.'"

We were the only persons present, except
the two men in charge of the burial. The
parents were strangers to almost every one,
having recently come among us.

The little coffin was laid upon the grass.
The undertaker took a key from his pocket,
opened the lid, and let it lean back.

The mother kneeled, and laid her hand on
the little breast, and bent over her child, with

expressions of love and grief which we could not but join to increase. The father was turning away, and was looking down into the grave, as though he had hurried to the very brink of the calamity, and was desperately in haste for the worst to come. I put my arm through his. "This will be a pleasant place," said I, "on the morning of the resurrection, to little George."

Mr. B. "There's room enough for us all three. I wish I was to be laid here with him."

Mr. M. "You are not ready yet, my dear sir; you must live, and believe in Christ, and do a great deal of good, and prepare to meet wife and child in heaven."

Mr. B. "They don't take such people as me there."

Mr. M. "But you will be a different man yet. 'The Lord gave and the Lord hath taken away;' try to say, 'and blessed be the name of the Lord.'"

Mr. B. "It's no use to say it, if you don't feel it."

R

Mr. M. "Oh, dear Mr. Burke, you will not quarrel with God at your little son's grave. I doubt not George is in heaven; he is perfectly happy, — happier than he could be here. No more trouble and sorrow, no more sin; he is safe, and Jesus has saved him. You will not leave him here. It is no more to him than though you were burying that little Scotchplaid frock and trousers, which my wife says he had on when she first saw him. God has done the very best thing which he could for you and George; you will not find fault with him. Could you see all the effects of this affliction, you might feel very much ashamed to blame God. He can make this thing the means of the greatest happiness to you.

"Besides," said I, "think what a great God he is. Look over this cemetery, and think how terrible his doings are. 'Behold, he taketh away! who can hinder him? Who can say unto God, What doest thou?' But 'he maketh sore and bindeth up; he woundeth and his hands maketh whole.' He has taken your little boy from you to heaven, and it almost distracts you. See how God can afflict us. Oh! let us make him our friend. 'Who hath hardened himself against Him and hath prospered?'"

Mr. B. "If them men will wait for us, I wish you would make a prayer."

"Oh! be as long as you please, sir," said the men, respectfully, while they withdrew and leaned over a rail-fence near by.

I told him that, if he wished for it, I would offer prayer. "You had better close the lid," said I, "while we pray; I am afraid the sight of the little face will prevent you from joining in prayer."

"Please don't shut it down tight," said the mother. "If we only had something to keep it a little ways open," said she, looking about her.

I took the tortoise-shell card-case and laid it edgewise, so as to keep the lid open about three inches. I had it in my heart to bless God that he had given me that card-case with its contents, it seemed such a privilege to use it in this way. How little did I ever think that it would come to such a scene, in which its possessor would be acting the part of comforter to the parents of a deceased only child, at that child's grave, in the same cemetery from which I first carried away the little key!

The grass was short and dry, the ground was safe to kneel upon, and we four kneeled around the coffin.

THE PRAYER.

" Will God look down upon us, as we come to render up this precious dust into his hands?

" 'I was dumb. I opened not my mouth, because thou didst it.'

" 'When thou with rebukes dost correct man for his iniquity, thou makest his beauty to vanish away like a moth. Surely every man at his best state is altogether vanity.'

" 'The Lord gave, and the Lord hath taken away ; blessed be the name of the Lord.'

"We have sinned against thee, and death is by sin, and so death passed upon all men, for that all have sinned.

"Thou art pleased to spare children, and make them a comfort to their parents; and again thou takest away, and none can stay thy hand, or say unto thee, 'What doest thou?'

"We know not which is best for us; we are short-sighted. Thou seest the end from the beginning, and hast in view every thing relating to each case, and thy decisions are wise and good.

"It is not for us to call in question thy wisdom in this event. We could have wished it otherwise; but the will of the Lord be done.

"Thou hast taken this little child to thyself, saved it by Christ. While we journey on, amidst darkness and tempests, with sins and sorrows, he will behold thy face, grow up to be like Christ, and come again at the last day to this grave, and receive a body like unto Christ's own glorious body. May we be comforted by this, and strive to have a part with him in that resurrection.

"May these dear parents remember that there is to be a meeting with their child, and that the question then will be, whether they are prepared for heaven. Let them not be separated from each other and from the child. Make its death the means of winning them both to God and heaven.

"Be pleased to sustain them in this hour of trial. May he who knelt in Gethsemane, and prayed that the cup might pass from him, remember them. May they remember him who then, for their sakes, said, 'Nevertheless, not as I will, but as thou wilt.'

"May they remember how many hearts have bled like theirs; that God has not sent upon them a greater trial than he has often prepared for others, and that he is able to turn it into the richest of blessings, by making them love and serve God.

"We now, in obedience to thy most holy will, commit this dust to the earth as it was.

We cling to it, we would keep it, but thou hast said, ' Dust thou art, and unto dust thou shalt return.' We bow before thy righteous mandate. In the name of Jesus, the Redeemer, forgive the sins which subject us to thy just displeasure here and hereafter.

"When they go back to their desolate home, comfort their hearts. May they not feel that they have left their child in the grave, but direct their thoughts to heaven : where their treasure is, there may their hearts be also.

"And now help us to take the last look, and go through the parting, with our eyes fixed on Christ, whom at the last day we expect to see in the clouds over this cemetery, coming to judge the living and the dead. May this grave not be a place of mourning to us then, but of rejoicing ; and meanwhile may our conversation be in heaven, where the dear child is, and where Jesus is, and where we shall be if we are followers of Jesus.

"And may the God of peace, who brought

again from the dead the Lord Jesus, that great
Shepherd of the sheep, through the blood of
the everlasting covenant, make us perfect in
every good work to do his will, working in
us that which is well pleasing in his sight,
through Jesus Christ, to whom be glory forever.   Amen."

We took up the body and buried it. We
saw the little mound made into shape; the
parents stood in silence over it, weeping
when a sudden clap of thunder, from a cloud
concealed by the hill near us, gave a new
direction to their thoughts, and led us to
hasten into the carriage from the storm.

Before we left the cemetery, the rain came
down, and the thunder and lightning were
terrific.

"I enjoy this," said I.

"You do?" said Mrs. B.: "I am always
afraid of being struck; but to-day I have no
fear."

"I wish we were safe at home," said Mr. B.

"I love to see and hear God in his works," said I:

> "'This awful God is ours,
> Our Saviour and our Friend.'

"How safe we are, Mr. B., with such a God on our side."

Mr. B. "O Mr. M.! I would give all the world to feel as you do about God."

Mr. M. "To lose a dear child, and then to feel rightly about it toward God, is among the surest means to make you love God. There is probably nothing that brings God and us nearer together than to lose a child; and now you will have the opportunity to show God what your feelings are toward him. Would you really love and serve God if you could?"

Mr. B. "That I would; for I begin to feel that I must have God on my side if I would be well off."

Mr. M. "There is one thing which I would give more to have you do than any thing else."

Mr. B. " I'll do any thing for you, sir, you've been so kind to us."

Mr. M. " But, oh! you do not know what it is. You will, I fear, refuse, and say you cannot do it; but you can if you will."

Mr. B. " Then I'll die but what I'll do it!" bringing his fist down upon his knee. " I always do what I set out for."

" Tell us what it is," said his wife.

" It is something," said I, " which will please Mrs. B. more than any thing you can do."

" Set up prayers," said she.

" Yes," I replied; " how came you to guess it ?"

" I've prayed for it ever since we kept house," said she. " Husband, did you hear ?"

" Mr. B.," said I, " after tea, take your Bible and read the twenty-third Psalm, and then kneel down with your wife, and pray to God."

He turned pale and red alternately; a mighty struggle arose within him; he pulled up the end of his frock-coat and gathered it into inch pieces, pressing them all together, then pulling the cloth out straight, entirely lost in thought, till at last he said, —

"Well, wife, I'll do it. I had my way about the baptism; now you shall have yours. If God will help me, I'll say something; but I don't know how to pray."

"We know not what to pray for as we ought," said I, "'but the Spirit itself maketh intercession for us with groanings which cannot be uttered.' The more you have of them, Mr. B., the more acceptably you will pray. God will understand it; for 'he that searcheth the hearts knoweth what is the mind of the Spirit, because he maketh intercession for the saints according to the will of God.'"

Mr. B. "Come over and pray with us, Mr. M., this evening, and help me, and we'll see what we can do."

After tea, I went in and read the Bible, and endeavored to lead the afflicted father to the Saviour of sinners. I then proposed to lead in prayer, and he engaged to follow. I prayed

much of the time, as in his name, making simple confessions and petitions. He followed,
in broken sentences, and evidently with a broken heart. I felt that the crisis was past;
that he had submitted himself to God; that,
as a lost and perishing sinner, he had accepted
Jesus Christ as his atoning sacrifice; and his
feelings with regard to the death of his child
were those of submission, though grief was
yet swelling within him in great billows; for
the sea had not gone down, though the moon
and stars appeared. He became a consistent
Christian, joined the church, took a seat in
the choir, he having a good, rich baritone
voice; and sometimes, when I have listened,
I could not be mistaken in the feeling that
the subduing influence of affliction had raised
him in the scale of being, and had opened sus-
ceptibilities in him which made him tenfold
more of a man than he was before, besides
enduing him, through grace, with that which
made him a new creature, and had changed
his prospects for eternity.

Several months after that, he called, with his wife, at my house, very respectably dressed, being now the owner of a provision stall in a large market, and in profitable business. His countenance was changed. It was refined, urbane, full of feeling; he was gentle and affectionate; he was a happy man.

"Do you know," said he, "what became of that key of ours the day we buried our little boy? Wife thinks that it was left in the lock."

"I brought it away with me," said I, "and have kept it safely. I thought that it would only harrow your feelings for me to give it to you there, so long as you had not spoken about it, and did not think to take it with you."

I brought it to him in a little box, which I had caused to be turned from a piece of an oak limb which had fallen from a tree in my lot in the cemetery, during a high wind. I had written the name of the child, with the dates of its birth, death, and burial, and it:

place of burial, on the ribbon. They looked
at it together, while different emotions chased
one another over their faces. He gave it
to his wife, who wrapped it in her handkerchief and placed it in her reticule, saying that
she believed the best thing that God had ever
done for her and her husband was to make
them the owners of that key.

CHAPTER IX.

THERE are some things which God does to us, perhaps, with the simple object of making us feel that he is God. Then a controversy arises between us and him, the issue of which is fraught with permanent consequences for good or evil in our characters and condition. If some in affliction could express all that they think and feel, they would tell us that they do not like the character and the doings of the Almighty, as they understand them. They would say, We cannot help this. Men make impressions on our minds according to their character and conduct. These impressions are involuntary. We do not feel complacency in the character of the Almighty, as we view it.

Such was the sad, the fearful state of mind in an infidel, as I was talking with him about the loss of his three children, who died within a year and a half of each other. His second child, a daughter of seventeen, was drowned in a pleasure-party; his oldest child, a son of nineteen, fell a victim to the cholera in a western city; and now his infant and his wife had just descended into one grave. The child, a week old, lay on its mother's arm in the coffin. Several hundreds of people had been to view the sight; and many a spectator grew faint as he felt the mighty hand of God in that dwelling, and said, "What desolations he hath made in the earth!"

It was toward sunset on Sabbath evening. I had been on an errand for a minister respecting the supply of his pulpit for the evening service, and was coming through one of the parks on my way home, when I met this bereaved husband and father strolling listlessly along, looking dejected and pale; and, when he saw me, he lifted his eyes without raising his head.

"Which way are you walking?" I said to him. He had formerly visited in my father's family, and we were on pleasant terms.

"Oh," said he, "nowhere; I came out to get away from myself, and from my tomb of a house. Sundays are awful things to a man like me."

"Well, now," said I, "Mr. Winn, I was praying for you last evening, if you will excuse me for speaking of it; for never in my life did I feel so toward a human being as I have felt toward you. Some lines of Crabbe have occurred to me in connection with your wife's untimely death: —

'Then died lamented, in the strength of life,
A valued mother and a faithful wife:
Not when the ills of age, its pains, its care,
The drooping spirit for its fate prepare,
But all her ties the strong invader broke
In all their strength, by one tremendous stroke.'" *

Taking out a little Bible which I always carry with me, I said, —

* The Sudden Death and Funeral. — *Crabbe's Tales.*

9

"In thinking of you last evening, I turned and read these words of Jeremiah in his Lamentations, which, it seemed to me, you could so appropriately use : —

"'I am the man that hath seen affliction by the rod of his wrath.

"'He hath led me and brought me into darkness, but not into light.

"'Surely against me is he turned; he turneth his hand against me all the day.

"'My flesh and my skin hath he made old; he hath broken my bones.

"'He hath builded against me, and compassed me with gall and travail.

"'He hath hedged me about, that I cannot get out; he hath made my chain heavy.

"'He was unto me as a bear lying in wait; and as a lion in secret places.

"'He hath turned aside my ways and pulled me in pieces; he hath made me desolate.

"'He hath bent his bow and set me as a mark for the arrow.

"'He hath caused the arrows of his quiver to enter into my reins.

"'He hath filled me with bitterness; he hath made me drunken with wormwood.

"'He hath also broken my teeth with gravel-stones; he hath covered me with ashes.

"'And thou hast removed my soul far off from peace ; I forgat prosperity.'

"You could hardly express your trouble in so many and such various terms, Mr. W. They all apply to you; and what a book the Bible is, containing every thing suitable to each case!"

He made no remark, and I added, —

"Job, too, was brought to my mind by your bereavements. All his children were cut off."

"Yes, but his wife was left. She was not much, I am inclined to think; yet he had somebody to talk to, and to be with him. I wander all over my house, and there is not

one place where I feel that I can sit down.
It is haunted by some association, or it seems
so lonely that I change the place but keep
the pain. O Mr. M.! if I had the manage-
ment of affairs, I would not excruciate mer
in this way."

"He doth not afflict willingly, nor grieve
the children of men," said I.

"Willingly or not," said he, "it is done;
and how can I think well of one who does
this? Now, I am a rational creature; I have
sense and reason; I am not a machine or
beast. I must judge of things as they are,
and I cannot bow my affections to a being
whom I cannot love. I suppose that I am
worse than people in general in this thing,
but I cannot help it; my feelings are involuntary."

"I do not think that you are worse than
people in general, by any means," said I, "in
having those feelings. Thousands have them
who do not express them as you do."

"Now," said he, "that is the only decent

thing which has been said to me for a fort·
night past. My relations are all Presbyte
rians, church-going people, and they think
me a regular blasphemer."

"But," said I, "it is a poor compliment to
say that you are no worse than thousands
who, like you, have a carnal mind, which is
enmity against God; for it is not subject to
his law, neither indeed can be."

"That is rather plain language," said he.

"You certainly are not the man to be of-
fended at the truth, Mr. W., after uttering
yourself as plainly as you have to me respect·
ing the Most High!"

"Did I say," said he, "that I was an enemy
to God? I take it that I may feel repugnance to a character, and yet not be an
enemy to the man who bears it."

I replied, "If a man thoroughly dislikes
his wife, with a settled aversion, is not his
mind enmity to her? Yet you would not
call him her enemy. But suppose a man to
be utterly opposed to the measures of a king,

and that he refuses to submit to him, and neglects every duty toward the government, talks to others against it, and his actions are in opposition to it; is he not justly called an enemy of the king? Surely he would be treated as such, under whatever name he might be arraigned."

" He might not be a personal enemy to the king," said he.

" As to all purposes of loyalty he is a rebel," I replied. " How remarkable it is that Christ sums up the whole moral law in this: Thou shalt love the Lord thy God, and thou shalt love thy neighbor. God makes religion, that is, our duty, to consist in, and flow from, love. Would it have satisfied you had that dear son of yours written to you, saying, ' Father, I am not your enemy, but I feel an utter repugnance to you? I do not, and I cannot, love you'? What if you should have said to your wife, ' Let us separate; I am not your enemy, but I totally disapprove of your principles and conduct, and take no pleasure in you.' All this you feel toward God."

"Well, I know I do," said he; "and a man may be perfectly justified in feeling so toward his wife, and a son toward his father."

"Justified," said I, "if the characters of the father and the wife are really such as these alienated minds assert. Allow that, in the judgment of competent people without number, they are, on the contrary, eminently lovely and good, what would that prove as to the son and the husband?"

"It would prove that men differ honestly about the same things," said he.

I replied, "If a little child at table says, 'Mother, my milk is sour,' and the mother tastes it and finds it perfectly sweet; and, the child still insisting that it is sour, the mother hands it to two or three grown people, and they also say it is perfectly sweet, what then?"

"Why," said he, laughing, "either the child's taste is out of order, or its temper."

"Mr. Winn," said I, taking the tortoise-shell card-case out of my pocket, and drawing forth

the little key, " there is the key of my little
daughter's coffin, as lovely a child as ever drew
the breath of life.   My child! my child! God
took her away from me.   Your children and
your wife were your all.   Agnes and my wife
were my joy; the child is dead, and my wife
is hastening after her.   The bitter sorrow
awaits me which you have drunk to the full.
How does this make me feel toward God ?"

"I should like to hear," said he, interrupting me.

"Mr. Winn," said I, "it makes me say,
'Whom have I in heaven but thee? and there
is none upon earth that I desire besides thee.
My flesh and my heart faileth, but God is the
strength of my heart and my portion forever.'"

"I presume you do not mean, by all that,
that you love him better than before ?"

"Better than before?" said I.   "There is
no comparison that does justice to the case; I
love him, I worship him, I serve him, so far
as my desires are concerned, as I never did.

'Though He slay me, yet will I trust in him.'"

"It is a mystery to me," said he, "and I suppose it is to you. It must be what you call sovereignty, or election, — something over which you have no control."

"Why," said I, "you said just now, speaking of yourself, 'I am a rational creature; I have sense and reason; I am not a machine nor a beast.' Will you allow me to be the same in these respects as yourself?"

"Then," said he, "how does it happen that you and I view the same things in such a totally different light?"

"Neither you nor I, nor any other man," said I, "is the standard of truth. There is a common standard, — the Word of God."

"I wish I had more confidence in it," said he, interrupting me.

"How improbable it is, Mr. W.," said I, "that a benevolent God would leave his creatures without some common standard of truth, which would be the arbiter among their con-

trary judgments and moral sentiments. This
argument in favor of a divine revelation con-
vinces me that the Bible is the Word of God.
He who gave us the magnetic needle, he who
has made the human hand, and the eye, with
such wise and benevolent adaptedness to our
wants, would not, he could not, fail to supply
us with such a means of instruction and comfort as a revelation from himself. He knew
that the greatest desire of his creatures would
be, to have authentic information of the character and the wishes of the Being who holds
them at his will, and of the way to please him,
— to say nothing of other things, which would
make a revelation indispensable. There must
be such a revelation, Mr. W. Did not the
astronomers, witnessing the perturbations of
Uranus, say, ' There must be a planet beyond
him to account for these disturbances ' ? Did
they not calculate where the undiscovered
world must be, and settle its distances, and
weight. and orbit, by rules which required all
which they afterward discovered ? I say that

such a system as that under which men live requires that there be a divine revelation, if there be a benevolent God."

" Oh," said he, " you go too fast and too far. I have not settled the point that there is such a benevolent Being."

" My dear friend," said I, " you cannot mean that your sufferings counterbalance all those proofs which Dr. Paley, for example, in his Natural Theology, quotes from every side to show the goodness of God ? If you are an exception to the general law of goodness, let it be so, and account for it in a rational way ; do not impugn the wisdom and goodness of God in the whole structural economy of animate and inanimate things."

" How shall I account for it, then, that I am an exception ? " said he.

" I deny that you are," said I. " You could not count up the number of those who have suffered as much as you. That peculiar trials should have fallen to the lot of any is to be explained hereafter, and not perhaps in this life ; and an old writer says, ' Quarrel not with God's unfinished providences.' You have no doubt that your wife and little child have gone to heaven?"

He made no reply.

" Your other daughter, too, I learn, was a Christian. Suppose your son, also, to have been prepared to die ; and suppose, now, that you could look in upon your whole family in heaven, would you feel that some great calamity had happened to them? Might not some there say, What family is this? Whom has God loved and honored so, that he has trans-. ferred them together here? There they are, a constellation of four stars in the firmament of heaven, known by some name, perhaps, and as beautiful to spectators as the Southern Cross, or Pleiades, with a vacant place in their arrangement waiting for you."

" That makes my present loss and pain no less," said he.

" But," said I, "seventy years are a small part of our whole existence. God may have judged that the very best way to secure your usefulness here, and your eternal happiness, was to take all your family to heaven. There you may see that the greatest kindness God ever bestowed upon you was to bereave you, and thus to keep you from having your portion in this life. He broke up your nest, and took you on his wings, and bore you abroad. He is now seeking to win your confidence and affection, that he may save you. Are you aware, my dear sir, that God loves you?"

" He cannot be what you say he is, if he can love me," said Mr. W.

" Because he is what he is, he loves you with infinite compassion; but not, of course, with complacency. His feelings towards you are those of infinite benevolence. You will be as welcome to his favor and to eternal happiness as any man. I am persuaded that the peculiarity of your afflictions is a proof of peculiar regard for you; God is making peculiar efforts to save you. Do not frustrate them. These clouds may be full of mercy.

How much your family in heaven must love
you! How must that dear wife long to show
you the little babe, which, under her tuition
in heaven, has become perfect in beauty!
Oh, can you bear to think of being separated
from them forever, Mr. W.?"

"I don't see but I must," said he, "if all
you say is true."

"No one but yourself will be to blame if
you are not saved," I replied. "God has used
the severest method to detach you from
earth. He now admonishes you, by what
you have suffered, that future and endless
separation will be intolerable. Speaking to
the Israelites, he tells them of their sufferings
when they shall be separated from their children by enemies in war. 'Thy sons and thy
daughters shall be given unto another people,
and thine eyes shall look and fail with long-
ing for them all the day long.' How insup-
portable home-sickness is to a husband and
father in a foreign land, thinking that the
ocean lies between him and his home! What

weariness and restlessness you feel now, as
you miss your wife and children! The world
is a sepulchre to you. What would you do
hereafter, to find that they are together in
heaven, and you banished from them?"

"Well, I wish that I had not been born,"
said he; "and, if there were such a thing as
annihilation, I would soon find it."

"Better be a happy spirit in heaven
through eternity, as you may be," said I.
"The time will come when you will look on
all these troubles with a peaceful mind. I
love to say those words to myself: 'Thou
which hast showed me great and sore troubles,
shalt quicken me again, and bring me up
again from the depths of the earth. Thou
shalt increase my greatness, and comfort me
on every side.' I shall not wonder if I see
you settled again, in a happy home, your feelings mellowed and chastened by affliction,
and you in possession of rich joys, and exert-
ing great influence by reason of your experience. God 'maketh sore and bindeth up; he

woundeth and his hands make whole. He
shall deliver thee in six troubles; yea, in
seven there shall no evil touch thee.'"

He began to wipe his eyes and to smile,
as he said, " Hope is a blessed medicine, after
all; Pandora shut down the lid of her box in
good time when she kept Hope behind, after
she had let out all our plagues."

" That is a good fable," said I; " but there
is a better Scripture for you : 'Now the God
of hope fill you with all joy and peace in
believing, that ye may abound in hope through
the power of the Holy Ghost.' What a name
that is, Mr. W., ' the God of hope.' "

" I am glad I met you," said he. " I begin
to think that I have been very foolish.
There's no use in being so stubborn. I
have stood in my own light. If I had done
better, I might have escaped these troubles."

" I am glad to hear you bemoaning yourself," said I. " Now turn to God, my dear sir,
humble yourself to him ; for he is God and
you but dust. ' Humble yourselves, therefore,

under the mighty hand of God, that he may exalt you in due time.'"

"Whether he exalts me or not," said he, in a somewhat excited way, which startled me, "you have made me feel that I have a duty to perform. Walk in," said he, as we came to his door. He rang the bell. A middle-aged woman opened the door a little ways, and peeped out, knowing that she was alone in the house, and feeling suspicious of every one who came to it.

"I want you to go with me," said he, "to the spot where my wife died."

The chamber was a little darkened, the blinds being partly shut. The full bed, with its snowy white drapery, had an affluent look. The door of the cedar-wood closet stood open, and there hung a lady's dresses, making me start at the thought of my intrusion into such a sanctuary; while I remembered, too, what mournful relics they were to this bereaved man. A little feature in a sad scene fre-quently occupies the chief place in our

10

thoughts, and here my eye was caught by the sleeve of a dress which hung out, with the bend in it made by the wearer's arm! How sick at heart did I feel; and what I should say to my friend in my frame of mind, I did not know, when I was surprised by the sound of his voice in prayer.

I looked round, and he was at the farther side of the bed, kneeling, and lifting up his folded hands upon the white coverlid. I shall never forget his words. I stole round and knelt at some distance from him, while he said,—

"O God, it is all right. I am a sinner. I am glad that there is One who is mightier than I am, and has conquered me, a rebel, and brought me to his feet. Oh, how much it took to bring me down! It is all right; I yield: do with me what seems good. For the blessed Jesus' sake, have mercy on a poor, desolate, lost, miserable sinner. Please do not let me suffer so forever. Save me from myself. Oh, my wife! my wife! my children! I never prayed with them. I might have ruined them if they had lived. God! thou hast snatched them away from their wicked father ; and now, oh, if God means to save the father too — what a God he must be, and "—

Here he fell into incontrollable sobbing, and buried his face in the side of the downy bed.

After a while I ventured to follow him in prayer, commending him to the infinite Friend and Saviour of sinners, leading him in my supplications to the Lamb of God which taketh away the sin of the world.

I shall always believe that, in that moment, he was reconciled to God through the death of his Son. On that spot, where his wife ascended to glory, he found eternal life, so that I said with myself, "'How dreadful is this place ! this is none other than the house of God, and this is the gate of heaven.'"

"Mr. M.," said he, "I shall sleep here to-night. I have always been afraid to come into the room. Now I should love to spend my days and nights here. Oh, what a God he is ! Do you think he can forgive and for-

get all my wicked words against him? When
he has been trying to do the very best thing
for me, what a shame that I should be treat-
ing him so. How is it that he spares men
who act as I did? Oh, if I don't spend my
life in making people love him! How came
he to send you to me in the Park? You
must have had a revelation. It could not
have been an accident. Let me see that card-
case again. That little key fitted the lock on
my heart, and you got into it. How old was
she? Do tell me all about her."

We were summoned down to his tea-table,
though I had already taken tea before leaving home. The table was beautifully and
richly spread.

"These initials on this china have an interesting tale, I suppose, to you," said I.

"Mr. M.," said he, "I am in a new world.
Every thing is changed. When I took up
these sugar-tongs and saw these embossed initials of my wife's name, a pang went through
me; but it was followed, for the first time, by

a feeling of peace, and even of joy. I have
something to live for now. God is better
than family, heaven is more than earth; to
do good is all that life is worth. Do help me,
and set me at work. Have you not some
poor people that I can visit? If any of them
are in trouble, let me know it. Excuse me;
you asked about the china,— I hardly think
of any thing that belongs to this world. Yes,
it came from Hamburg, a wedding present
from her mother; but how it has lost its value
to me in a day! How little she cares for it!
What are all these treasures worth? I have
property, you know; but it could not give
health nor save life. My house is full of val-
uable things, and now I should be willing to
give them all away and be a missionary, if I
were fit. Do tell me every thing about that
little key. I suspect, by your carrying it
with you, it has had some great effect upon
your feelings. Now I think of it, I know that
undertaker has one that belongs to me. Yes,
it was locked, I am sure," said he, with a

thoughtful inclination of his face; "the coffin was locked before I came out of the tomb, I remember. I heard the little click. I must go to-night, — no, it's the Sabbath, — I will go to-morrow, and get that key."

"Do so," said I. "You will find it to be the richest and most useful treasure, next to the Bible, which ever came into your hands." And after much conversation I bade him good-night.

"God bless you, my dear sir," said he. "Do not regret leaving me alone now; the house seems full of God. You have done good to one miserable sinner; keep on, and God help you to bless many like me."

What a walk was that to my house! I took the little key and bathed it with kisses and tears. Dear little Agnes! you have done great good already by your death. "O Lord, our Lord, how excellent is thy name in all the earth, who hast set thy glory above the

heavens.   Out of the mouth of babes and
sucklings hast thou ordained strength because
of thine enemies, that thou mightest still the
enemy and the avenger."

CHAPTER X.

VISITING some friends, I found a man who had often conversed with me about a great affliction which had happened to him eighteen months before.

He had long been dejected, had separated himself from the world, and spent much time in reading the Bible and in prayer.

He told me that all this seclusion and seeming devotion had no good effect upon him; but the contrary. He, too, had lost a child, and then his wife. It had made him almost insane. The loneliness of his situation was his greatest affliction, on account of the brooding melancholy which it occasioned. Unhappily, he was obliged to follow a sedentary life, being a very able accountant, and spending his time at home over books and sheets of figures, which were deposited with him by assignees. He was a man of education, of great refinement, of taste and feeling, and in easy circumstances.

The day that I called to see him, I was surprised to find him unusually cheerful and happy. I expressed my wonder, and asked him if any thing good had happened to him.

"Sit down here on this sofa," said he, "and I will tell you all about it. You know that I have been in the depths of misery ever since I met with my bereavement. How much I have prayed over it I cannot tell you. Never was it out of my thoughts for many moments at a time. It would come over me suddenly while adding up a column of figures, and put every thing out of my mind. I could not forget her, nor my dreadful agony when she died, and at the funeral and the grave. Oh, how I have prayed to God, day and night, that he would relieve me! Sometimes, however, I have kneeled down to pray about it, and all

my feeling seemed to depart. I was as dead
and cold as a stone. I began to understand
what Coleridge describes, —

> ' A grief without a pang, void, drear, and dark,
>   A stifled, drowsy, unimpassioned grief,
>   Which finds no natural outlet and relief,
>   In word, or sigh, or tear.' *

" I said a few incoherent words, and went
away, feeling that I had no religion, reproach-
ing myself that I could treat my Maker in
such a manner. Then I would relent and
again ask God to comfort me; but praying
only seemed to make my sensibilities more
keen, and to press my bitter loss upon them.

" One evening, as I was kneeling and praying about it, and finding that I was going
through the same process which for so long a
time had resulted in disappointment, it suddenly struck me that I must help myself. I
had a feeling of resolution come over me,
which I think was in answer to prayer. I
resolved that I would no longer be such an

* Dejection. — *Coleridge's Poems.*

impotent creature. I plainly saw that God could not help me except as he made me help myself, and I resolved to use means of relief in dependence on God.

"The first thing I did was to accept an invitation to a select party, made in honor of some friends of mine. I had shut myself out from all such scenes for more than a year; and now, though I had no more relish for them than before, I resolved that I would mix with society, not to be entertained, but to make others happy. I went to the party with that resolution. It was, some would think, an incongruous thing to go to a party under the influence of a text; but why should it be so? I thought of this: 'The Son of man came not to be ministered unto, but to minister.' That evening I spoke with almost every one in the room. Those whom I did not know, I asked to be made acquainted with, and exchanged pleasant words with them; found that some of them were old acquaintances of my parents, and some went to school with my sisters; and

some told me what frolics they and I had
when we were children together, and others
related their great sorrows: till at last I found
that I was really a happy man, — younger by
ten years than a day before. I saw some of
them look at me, and overheard one say to
another, ' What do you suppose has happened ?
Engaged again ?' I went home resolved that
I would no longer live to myself. When I
went to my room that night, the first thing I
did was to repent of my thousands of prayers.
How selfish, how wrong, they seemed. Oh,
how God must have regarded me, a droning,
morbid creature, refusing to do and to enjoy
any thing because I had been afflicted, and
asking God to do an impossibility! I never
before truly submitted myself and my trouble
to God; my prayers were complaints, mur-
murings, if not impeachments; but I began
to see and feel the power of that word, ' Be
still, and know that I am God.' I do believe
that the best help which we can have in affliction is that which, by God's grace, we are

enabled to give ourselves, using our common
sense, availing ourselves of expedients to
assist and cheer the mind, resorting to various methods of changing the current of
thought, making waste-locks and weirs to
diminish the strength of tide, and seeking
supplies of new thoughts and feelings for our
help."

"Had you no alternations of feeling?" said
I. "Did not your sorrows come back without
leave?"

"Of course they did," said he; "but I took
care to barricade myself against them. Short
journeys I found useful; entertaining, cheerful books, especially those of a scientific,
descriptive kind, which led to no intro-
verted contemplation, but kept my thoughts
out at pasture; humorous writings, the news
of the day, any thing which would take my
attention and hold it by an intrinsic interest,
so that I did not feel that I was practising arts
with myself, did much to help me."

"But did you not thereby lose something

of your spiritual-mindedness, your interest in prayer?"

"Far from it. My prayers became more like the Epistle of James; works and faith met in them; I had a good conscience; I was living to make others happy; I had become reconciled to God. Besides, I had more true religious enjoyment than before, from Scriptural truths."

"That is what I should be glad to hear you speak of more at large," said I; "for whatever illustrates the Word of God is exceedingly precious."

"Well," said he, "one day I read this passage: 'The night is far spent, the day is at hand.' It came to my mind, How soon I shall be in heaven! Perhaps even now I am on the very verge; perhaps in a few days I shall be with God. How sorry I shall be if I spent my time in useless weeping, when relief was all the while so near.

"I thought also of these words: 'If thou faint in the day of adversity, thy strength is small.' It is sublime to bear the fearful strokes of God's providence with meekness and firmness; to endure; to show one's self a man. How true this is: —

  ' God did anoint thee with his odorous oil,
   To wrestle, not to reign.' *

"I have felt that terrible calamities are great blessings to the spirit of a man who knows how to suffer. To such a man, a great affliction from God is like a great blast in a quarry, — it throws out great treasures, or it opens a way for great projects. I revere a man who is in great affliction. God seems to have selected him, like a piece of second-growth timber, for an important work. It is not every one who can be trusted to suffer greatly. I look with great respect upon an honest man who has fallen into disfavor and is greatly abused. Many a time, when we were boys, you know, we were attracted to an apple-tree in a pasture, by the great number

* Mrs. Browning. — " What are we set on earth for ? "

of clubs and stones which lay under it, showing that the fruit had attracted notice. To
angels in heaven, a good man enduring sufferings well must be a sublime sight, for sufferings and faith are no part of their experience ; but to see a mortal bearing the afflic-
tive hand of God with faith and love, must
excite their admiration. How angels flocked
around Christ! how they must have loved
him when at the end of his temptation
'the devil leaveth him, and, behold, angels
came and ministered unto him!' There
is the truest courage, I think, in adjusting
ourselves to our circumstances. If God be-
reaves us, let us live bereaved ; if he takes a
blessing from us, let us do without it; not
with stoicism, but with childlike submission:
'Father, you know best.'

"Besides," said he, "God is all the time
teaching us that this is not an unmixed condition, neither of evil nor good. Compensa-
tions are the rule of his gracious providence;
we all have them. I have learned to have

less pity for greatly afflicted people than formerly; for I know that they have great consolations, and their losses are in one way and another atoned for, in some degree, if they feel and act right. 'In the day of prosperity be joyful; but in the day of adversity consider: God also hath set the one over against the other, to the end that man should find nothing after him,' making man feel that God adjusts and disposes every thing. These lines of Gray have been a comfort to me : —

> 'Still, where rosy pleasure leads,
>   See a kindred grief appear;
>   Behind the steps that misery treads,
>   Approaching comfort hear.
>   The hues of bliss more brightly glow
>   Chastised by sadder tints of woe,
>   And blended, form, with artful strife,
>   The strength and harmony of life.' " *

"Now," said I, "let me thank you for all that you have said, and tell you something of my experience under sorrow, and that may

---

* Vicissitude. — *Gray's Poems.*

start other trains of thought in you which I shall be glad to hear."

"I have heard several speak of that little key of yours," said he, "and what legerdemain you seemed to work with it in the feelings of people. I hope that you will try it on me."

"You are past needing it," said I; "yet we can always help one another from our expe rience. One effect of affliction on me has been to make me forgiving. People sometimes inflict great injuries upon me; for you know my calling leads me into scenes where I have to resist the evil passions of men. Few men get more ill-will than one who tries to discharge the duties of his place with im partiality. The treatment which I used to meet with frequently embittered my feelings against men. Since I lost my child, strange to say, I find it harder to cherish animosities. Some weeds, you know, cannot take hold of rich soil; they need sandy, coarse ground; so, when our hearts are fertilized by affliction.

it is hard for certain poor things to get a place
there. When a man injures me, I have a
feeling of tenderness towards him come over
me at times, if I say with myself, I wonder if
he has a little child, or ever lost one; and
that thought — you will smile — has sometimes kept me from replying in the newspa-
pers to angry assaults upon me. I know how
weak many would deem me for this; but so
it is. Many a time, when my feelings have
been exasperated, I have taken the little key
into my hands, and the thought of the little
grave has calmed my passions. I have stolen
Mark Antony's words, —

> 'My heart is in the coffin there with' Agnes,
> 'And I must wait till it comes back to me.'

As, when it thunders and lightens, I often
think how secure the little sleeper is; and,
when the heavy rain comes down on that
peaceful bed, my heart betakes itself to calm
thoughts, because the precious dust feels no
tempests, wakes at no alarm, — so in trouble

that little grave makes me feel peaceful. How often have I said to myself, when a man has written against me or spoken ill of me, Could I meet him at the grave of his little child or mine, we should almost love one another; we should write and speak about each other, publicly, in unexceptionable terms. I almost wish that some of our great conventions could be held inside the fences of some cemetery."

"There will be a great convention in every one of them, one of these days," said he. "The last great meetings of men on earth will most of them be held there."

"Each of us will come to attend them," said I.

"Resolutions will be of no effect then," he added, taking up a newspaper filled with matters relating to the presidential election. "Oh, did you notice the loss of that passenger ship with four hundred souls on board?"

"I did, and it made me think, What a cemetery is the sea! None are thought of, loved,

and mourned over more than they who find
their sepulchre there. It is soothing to have
the dust of a child or friend in a sure, safe
grave, when you meet with those whose
loved ones are lost in the great waters. But
He who is the resurrection and the life has
his eye upon them. The Lord buried them,
and no man knoweth of their sepulchres.
And yet they are more conspicuously buried
than those on land. Few know where one
and another on land lies buried, but the un-
known sepulchre of the deep is well known;
those viewless graves are ever before our
eyes. I have noticed that they who are lost,
or die, at sea, exert great religious influence
on survivors at home. Christ is magnified in
their bodies by their death.

"I love to think," said he, "that our sepa-
rations, griefs, and our improvement under
them, will make us love each other intensely
when we meet again."

I said to him, "If afflictions make us sullen,
slothful, jealous of God, morose, and useless,

we shall feel very much ashamed hereafter.
Our afflictions pierce the heart of God before
they reach ours. He is willing to see us suffer greatly for the endless good effect which
he means to accomplish by it. Should he
spare the rod for our crying, or should he
consult our wishes, it would be our calamity."

"Do you not suppose," he asked, "that the
remembrance and the pain of some trials follow us to the end of life? When I was sick
some years ago, they gave me a medicine
which they called Hiera Picra, which, trans-
lated, you know, means Sacred Bitter. God
seems to dispense such medicines sometimes.
I could not remove the taste of that bitter
by any expedient."

"Do you remember," I inquired, "a passage
in Prior's Life of Edmund Burke, which
speaks of his feelings at the loss of his son,
the ' low moan ' which continued in his heart
long after he had submitted to God, and how
he would hang on the neck of his son's horse
and weep? Yes, there are sorrows which we

carry with us to our graves. They ought,
however, to make us more useful, more diligent, more grateful for redemption; for what
must it be to ' lie down in sorrow,' in another
world? To a man in hell, what `must the
recollection of his children be? What a
word that is, ' Ye shall *lie down* in sorrow '!
Did you ever notice that fearful imprecation,
' Give them sorrow of heart, thy curse unto
them ' ? "

" My heart exults sometimes," said he, " in
thinking of that word, ' And God shall wipe
away all tears from their eyes; and there
shall be no more death, neither sorrow, nor
crying, neither shall there be any more pain;
for the former things are passed away.' We
can bear any thing for this short period; the
thought that afterward there is never to be
one sensation of pain or grief, but increasing
bliss forever, ought to make us cheerful here."

" It ought to make us diligent," I replied;
" for when I think how long that bliss will be,
how many are in danger of losing it, how

short a time we have to secure it, and help others to obtain it, I do not feel impatient for heaven; I wish to live and do good to my fellow-men."

As we parted, I told my friend how glad I felt that he had learned the self-control which religion teaches. Our feelings are not given to us for our guide; we must subject them to the laws of God. Though it was easier to commend him than fully to imitate him, I carried away with me a new purpose, that, by the help of God, I would endeavor, more than ever, to help myself.

CHAPTER XI.

"Which is the greater trial," said my wife as we rode home from a visit to some friends in affliction, — "to lose a child, or to leave it?"

I replied, "To lose it, so far as my observation has gone. Nothing has surprised me more than the resignation and peace of some Christian mothers, when called to die and to leave a family of young children. There was a pang when the conviction that they must die came over them; but it was short, and I have wondered at the self-possession with which they looked upon the children afterwards."

Mrs. M. "How do you account for it?"

Mr. M. "Partly from natural causes. Some instincts which are given us for self-

preservation are mercifully suspended when
they can be of no use. People falling from
a height, or thrown from a vehicle, are not
fully sensible of what is happening to them.
Besides, God is pleased to stay his rough wind
in the day of his east wind. Dying grace is
for a dying hour; we cannot feel in health
as we shall in the last hours of life."

Mrs. M. "The expectation of what is to
happen to ourselves, I suppose, abates our
solicitude for others."

Mr. M. "When I had made up my mind
to go to Europe, after we were married, the
anticipation of all which I was to see and experience held my regret at leaving you, so to
speak, in suspension; the mind cannot long
be acted upon powerfully by two opposite
passions: one yields; and so I suppose it is
with the solicitude of parents for their children, when their own departure takes full
possession of their thoughts. But there is
something better than all this, I think, as a
means of preparing us to leave children."

Mrs. M. " What is that?—for I am going this afternoon to see Mrs. Wales, who is dying of consumption. She has six children, from sixteen down to one year old."

" I will go with you," said I ; " for I should expect to be greatly instructed by seeing and hearing her."

The morning-glories were climbing over the windows of Mrs. Wales's humble room, turning their simple, beautiful trumpet-flowers, of different colors, in all directions, and some of them towards the open window, where I took my seat.

" God is here, my dear Mrs. Wales," said I, as I drew one of the creepers toward me, full of flowers, and looked at her. " If God so clothe the grass, how much more will he clothe you."

She was supported in bed with pillows, looking nearly as white as they. The peace of God which passeth all understanding was expressed in her face.

" Mr. M.," said she, " I have given all up to

God, and feel that I no longer have any responsibility for any thing."

My wife asked her if she was able to look upon her babe and the other children with composure of mind.

"Yes," she replied; "but I am a wonder to myself. Their father has gone to heaven, and I expect to be there soon, and these children will be orphans. But I have this feeling: God knows what he is doing. Now, if he sees fit to take us away from our six children, let him do it; for he sees a reason for it which would satisfy me, could I be made acquainted with it. Or, if he never tells me why he does it, still, blessed be his name; for who are we, that God should explain his conduct to us? Oh, how good it is to trust God and love him, when you cannot understand his ways!"

Mrs. M. "But you must have some natural pangs, as you think of parting with these dear ones."

Mrs. W. "O Mrs. M.! there is no reasoning about it. All I know is that I am at peace."

Mr. M. "Tell me, Mrs. Wales, what one thought comes to your mind with special power as you think of leaving these children? Is there one thing more than another which gives you special comfort?"

Mrs. W. "I think it is this: I feel sure of meeting them all in heaven, and it seems to me a very little while ere I shall. The last time I went to church, our minister was speaking about the expectation which the Apostles sometimes seem to have had, that the day of the Lord was near, and he said perhaps it might be accounted for by their all-absorbing interest in that event, which made intervening time and objects shrink to nothing. Heaven and eternity so engross my mind, that I strangely forget earthly things, however important; and I chide myself sometimes for not planning and directing about my children. But, besides being weak, I stop myself when I do this at all, by saying, How little you know

about the future! It is like walking in the
fog. You can see a few steps only at a time;
take them, and you can see as many more.
My sister and her husband have promised to
befriend my children; but, oh!" said she, covering her face, "God is their God and my God,
— that is enough."

Mr. M. "But you feel so sure of meeting
them all in heaven, — how is this? What
gives you such confidence?"

Mrs. W. "Jane, my child, hand Mr. M.
that missionary paper which has the piece
about leaving children."

It was a periodical of a foreign missionary
society. I read aloud. It seems that a dying
father, a missionary, was about to leave four
young children; his wife, their mother, having
previously died. The writer says:

"There was another subject which claimed his most earnest
thought. He was about to leave his four motherless children,
in a strange land, to the exclusive care of a doubly-bereaved
sister. Knowing him to be an affectionate father, always
anxious and careful in regard to his offspring, I hardly dared to
mention the case. I soon found, however, that his mind was

entirely at rest in relation to them. Their sainted mother had dedicated them to God; he had renewed that dedication. A covenant had been made with the Lord to train them up wholly for him. But now, by his holy providence, one party (the parents) was disabled from performing the covenant; its whole execution, therefore, devolved upon God. He is faithful and almighty; not one thing which he has promised shall fail. Our dying brother triumphed in this thought. He said he felt sure that he should meet all his children in heaven. 'Sumner, Ellen, Lizzie, and (his voice failing, he rallied his waning powers, and, conquering the conqueror, said clearly) Susie! Not one of them will be wanting.' He thus left them with the most delightful and unreserved confidence in the care of a covenant-keeping God and a gracious Father. Knowing his anxious temperament, I looked with wonder and admiration upon this victory of his faith."

Mrs. W. "That is my expectation and my hope. God is a covenant-keeping God. I have intrusted my soul to him for eternity in Jesus Christ, and I will trust my children with him."

Mrs. M. "Have you no doubt, Mrs. W.?"

Mrs. W. "Sometimes it is whispered in my ear, The children of good people do not always turn out well; yours may be of that description. I cannot reason about this, either; for,

‘ Where reason fails
With all her powers,
There faith prevails,
And love adores.

"You have lost your dear child," said she ;
"you are not to leave her behind you.   Some
might think that you have more to be thankful for than I.   It may not seem so hereafter.
When my six children come to me in heaven,
having been useful here, bringing their sheaves
with them, how glad I shall be that I had six
orphans to trust with God ?"

I did not take out the little key from my
pocket, as I thought at first that I should do.
These words had made me feel that some of
my sorrows over that little key had not been
wise.   I saw that it would be out of place if I
should use it to instruct this dying saint.

"Beautiful words," she continued, — "‘ the
seed of Abraham, my friend.'   Have you never
witnessed, Mr. M., touching instances of kindness among men towards the children of one
who was an early friend ?"

Mr. M. "Surely I have. I am myself an instance of it. A friend of my father, who grew up with him, has bestowed loving kindness on me which I can never repay in this world."

Mrs. W. "Is not God the author of that feeling towards the child of a dear friend?"

Mr. M. "No doubt he is."

Mrs. W. "Then he possesses it himself."

Mr. M. "Yes, and exercises it, he says, 'to a thousand generations.'"

"Mrs. Wales," said I, "the influence of a godly man or woman, eminent for some special love and service towards God, follows in the line of descent through long periods of genealogy; there are families among us, you know, who have a reputation for goodness; uncommon numbers of their children are hopefully pious; we honor the stock to which they belong, but we do not always consider that all has proceeded, in many cases, without doubt, from the signal favor which God bore to some man or woman who maintained a

12

life of peculiar walking with God, sealing it
continually with fresh acts of love and service.
And so that blessing promised to Christ is vir-
tually fulfilled to them : 'I will make thy
name to be remembered in all generations;
therefore shall the people praise thee for ever
and ever.' "

"But," said my wife, "what sight is more
heart-rending than a family of orphans?"

"And yet," said I, " observation has led me
to feel less and less solicitude, in seeing a family of children left in orphanage by parents
who were truly the children of God. The
self-reliance which they early learn and prac-
tise, the restraining and subduing power of a
deceased parent's memory, the friends raised
up for them, all afford a good comment on
those words, 'Leave thy fatherless children:
I will preserve them alive.' Nothing seems
to us more in violation of the natural and
proper order of things, than the removal of a
mother from a family of young children. We
would have provided against such a calamity

by a special law, had we arranged the affairs of life and death. He who is willing to do so great and solemn a thing as to remove a mother from the head of her large family must have reasons for it, as Mrs. Wales says, 'which would satisfy us, could we see them with a right mind.' Such an event is so peculiarly an act of God's providence, we may suppose that He who giveth to the beast his food, and to the young ravens which cry, will not fail to accomplish some great and good purpose by it to all who love him. He soothes the feelings of our dear Mrs. Wales, makes her speak words of comfort and cheer to those whom she is about to leave, and thus he secures for himself, in the hearts of the children, oftentimes, and in those of their friends, a degree of confidence in God as a covenant-keeping God, which nothing else could so well inspire."

Mrs. W. "I expect to do more for my children in heaven than I could if I should live."

Mrs. M. "Why, Mrs. Wales, we came here

to comfort you; but we are almost tempted to say we have never found so great faith, — certainly not in ourselves."

Mr. M. "Please tell us how you expect in heaven to influence your children."

Mrs. W. "They will cherish my memory; remember my words; say to themselves, How would mother approve or disapprove of this? They will never forget my praying with them. I have had scenes with each child which they will think of as long as they live."

A sweet girl of twelve years, standing with her face toward the window, began to sob, and suddenly left the room.

Mrs. W. "Oh, that dear Charlotte! I was about to punish her, when she was eight years old, for an untruth. I took her into my chamber, locked the door, kneeled with her, spread the case before God, asked him to help me punish her, and to bless the rod for her salvation, and then I administered the punishment. She did not cry, but as soon as I had done, she put her arms about me, and said, 'Dear mother, God has forgiven me ; will you ?' She has been almost a faultless child from that day to this. Discipline, Mr. M., is greatly needed in many Christian families,— the subjection of children, by proper restraints and punish. ments, to authority ; but they must be made to feel, in order to be benefited, that God is on the parents' side; and therefore I have found prayer to be a powerful help in correct. ing a child. I have not finished my work with my children; it will go on when I am in heaven."

Mrs. M. " I thought that you would say that you expected to minister to them here- after ; yet I know that you are not apt to have romantic or visionary feelings. What do you think about this ? "

Mrs. W. " I may or may not minister to them directly ; that will be as God sees fit. What could I do for them ? — I, who cannot save myself, and who will not be omniscient in heaven, any more than I am here, — what can I, or angels, do for my children, except as God appoints? I trust I shall not come between them and God, in their love and confidence; at least, I have told them so."

The young woman who took care of her brought in the little boy, about a year old. He saw his mother, and made his hands and feet fly in his eagerness to get to her. I looked at my wife, and saw her face covered with tears and smiles. I knew that she was reminded, by the child, of her own little girl, and of the different circumstances in her own case and that of Mrs. Wales; and that she was making comparisons between this dying mother and herself. Christian mother, which of the two would you prefer to be, — a bereaved mother, your little child in heaven, or a dying widow, leaving six children behind you?

If you say, a bereaved mother, perhaps one reason is, you have been bereaved, and would rather suffer known evils than those which your fancy depicts or thinks it sees in others.

But while, in the nature of things, it is a

greater trial of faith to leave a family of children, you probably never saw a parent doing
so who suffered as much as one who has buried
a child. O Death! there is, to survivors,
something in thee to which life, with all its
fears and burdens, furnishes no counterpart.
Thou art God's curse against sin, unrepealed
by all the consolations and hopes of religion,
which indeed help us to endure the stroke,
but do not make Death other than the king
of terrors to us, in his approaches to those
whom we love. It is not so hard for a Christian to die, under any circumstances, as it is
to lose a child or beloved companion. The
dying grace which we say is for a dying hour,
sustains us when we die and leave our friends;
but, when they or a child are taken from us,
we are left with all our weaknesses and sin-
fulness to suffer under the loss.

A pleasant sight now caught my eye. A
little girl, about three years old, had made
herself acquainted with my wife during this
call, and had been practising her little arch

ways of play with her. My wife had now
lifted her upon the bed where the mother
lay; she drew up her chair, fixed a napkin
on the child's bosom, and set her to eating
a delicious Bartlett pear, which she had in
her pocket. There are few things that afford
such a mixture of amusement and happiness
as to take a little child unawares, one with
whom you are on familiar terms, set it down,
and watch it, as you give it a delicious fruit
and see it eaten. The looks of pleasure from
a pair of roguish eyes, the glow of satisfaction overspreading the features, the laughter
mixing in with the motion of the face in eating, the occasional offer of a bite to the
mother, the slight embarrassment at seeing
us all looking at her, made the little girl the
object of delighted admiration; while the
thought of its approaching orphanage awak-
ened in us feelings of tenderness and love.

"I dare say," said her mother, "little Ra-
chel will meet with a great many kind acts, and
be taken care of. 'I know all the fowls of

the mountains,' God tells us. This little one
is of more value than many sparrows, isn't
she? I am going to be with God, and he
will remember my children, surely, when he
sees me; and, if he needed any remembran-
cer, how much better able I should be there,
to obtain help for them, than here. But, after all, how little we know about such things!
I give all up, and leave them with God.'

We walked away; and, so full were we of
what we had seen and heard, that we hardly
spoke to each other for several minutes. At
last I said, —

"From this time, I will certainly refrain
from sorrowing over our afflicted condition.
I would not exchange places with Mrs. Wales,
with all her consolations."

Mrs. M. "If you were in her place, you
would have her consolations with it. I am
not sure that I shall cease to sorrow. Our
loss is none the less real and great now than
before we made this call; only, we see how
wrong it is to think that our sufferings are
peculiar."

Mr. M. "One thing makes me feel humble and quiet. Here is a dear saint, whom (if he loves me at all) God loves as much as he loves me. Everywhere we can find those who are dear to him. It bids me refrain from exalting myself and my affairs in my own esteem. I am only one; there are other interests which are as important as mine; I feel sorry that I have dwelt so much on my affliction."

Mrs. M. "If it has not made us murmur, nor kept us from doing our duty, we ought not to reproach ourselves for our sorrows. If something had made us happy, how inconsistent it would have been if we had wept. God intends that we should be joyful in prosperity, and in adversity consider."

Mr. M. "It does me good to express my unconsidered feelings to you; for, by the act of expressing them, I am led to see their error, and so am kept from brooding over them."

Mrs. M. "You said nothing, I observed, to Mrs. Wales, about Agnes."

Mr. M. "How could I, with such a sight before me as those little children of hers, about to lose such a mother?"

Mrs. M. "One of the best helps in sorrow and trouble, surely, is to visit people in affliction."

Mr. M. "What scenes there must be in heaven, every day, in the meetings of parents and children, and relatives and friends! but, among them all, I do think that to meet a little child who died in infancy, and has been for years in heaven, must have as much of surprise and gladness in it as any thing."

Mrs. M. "Yes; but, after the surprise and gladness are over, there is something else which I think must be a richer and more permanent joy. You know that, when the novelty of meeting, after long separation, has ceased, we need something still to prevent satiety. Now, it seems to me that the greatest, the most enviable joy, in heavenly recognitions, must be experienced by those who themselves, or whose children, or companions,

or dear friends, have been eminently good and
serviceable to God and man. Much as I an-
ticipate in meeting Agnes, I cannot sympathize
with those parents who long to die in order to
see their children. After getting home and
finding all well, you know that life here runs
on as before; getting home is not every thing,
pleasant as happy returns are. I would rather
be Mrs. Wales in heaven, receiving her children who shall have borne the Saviour's cross
here, and hearing him say, ' Well done!' than
to meet dear little Agnes, a thousand times
over."

Mr. M. "You are right; so should I."

Mrs. M. "I wish there were less of selfish-
ness in our sorrows, and less of it in our ex-
pectations of heaven. To be useful is the
great end of life. God makes some useful to
his church by suffering; others by working.
There is that sick minister, whom we met at
S—— Springs, afflicted in such complicated
ways. One of his people told me that he had
done great good by his spirit and behavior in

trouble, and by his prayers and occasional
preaching, in all the neighboring churches.
His wife must rejoice over him, when he
comes to her in heaven, far more in conse-
quence of the way in which God has honored
him in doing good bv him, than for any other
reason."

Mr. M. "I am told that they send for him,
far and near, to visit people in great trouble of
mind. He is a son of consolation. A member of Congress told me that he could count
nine educated men, who, he thought, had been
led to a religious life by the personal influence
of that man."

Mrs. M. "Suppose that he had spent his
time only in weeping over his bereavements
and afflictions?"

Mr. M. "'He that goeth forth and weep-
eth, bearing precious seed,' — the weeping
sower seems to be a paradox in natural things;
but in spiritual things it is good for sowers to
be great weepers."

Mrs. M. "What is the rest of that passage?"

Mr. M. "'Shall doubtless come again with rejoicing, bringing his sheaves with him.'"

Mrs. M. "'Sheaves with him.'   That is the way to make meetings and greetings in heaven happy.   Just to be restored to lost friends, — how poor a satisfaction this is, of itself!   Happiness here needs something solid to make it satisfying ; it will be so there.   Oh, I hope, if you survive me, that you will not waste your time and strength in sorrowing, but remember how happy you will be, and how happy you will make me, if my death shall make you love God and the Saviour more than ever, and fit you to bless and help to save men.   Think how much good God has enabled dear little Agnes to do through us; what a happy eternity she will have, as she traces out the influences of her death far down, it may be, to the judgment day !   What is the mere pleasure of meetings and recognitions, compared with this ?"

But it becomes me here to draw the veil

and hide from view the "treasures of darkness" connected with an event which soon
followed this conversation. It was a little
coffin, and no other, that furnished the key
which has given occasion to this book.

And now the graves of Mother and Child
lie side by side in one of our cemeteries.
To one of the parents, therefore, the key
of the little coffin has ceased to be a memorial and a type, for the child is restored to
her embrace. I am now sole proprietor of
the little key. But as the evening star now
sets earlier daily, and hastens below the
horizon into the east, so the sad associations
with this little symbol make less and less im-
pression, and morning airs and dawning light
are taking their place. As I was last week
planting candy-tufts and the marvel-of-Peru
upon those graves, — varying, as I love to
do each year, the annuals or biennials which
grow there, and expecting, without fail, to see
flowers bloom from those seeds, — I thought of

what was planted underneath, and how certain it is that, in due season, I shall reap if I faint not.

I feel disposed to end my tale in keeping with a beautiful epitaph over a grave near Athens, in Greece, which is in these sweet words : —

EUBULUS,

SON OF LAON,

LIVED SEVENTEEN YEARS.

FAREWELL.

The "farewell" on the stone is to the reader, — a comely act of gentle behavior in sorrow to the stranger whose curiosity should lead him to approach that grave.

So, dear reader, farewell! Agnes lived a twelvemonth, and here is her story.

If God sees fit to use you in doing good, and would qualify you for great enjoyment, here and hereafter, he can accomplish it, perhaps, in no way more effectually than by putting into your hands the key of some precious, buried treasure. Again, farewell!